SHRUB

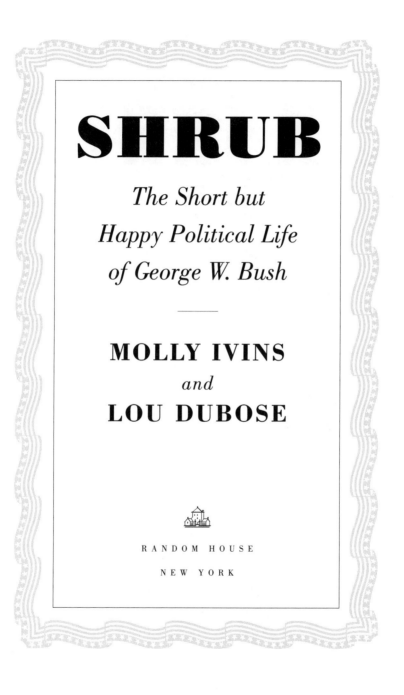

SHRUB

*The Short but
Happy Political Life
of George W. Bush*

MOLLY IVINS

and

LOU DUBOSE

RANDOM HOUSE

NEW YORK

Book design by Victoria Wong

This book is dedicated to *The Texas Observer* and to all who have sailed in her for forty-seven years. The scrappy little magazine covers Texas politics and social problems under the following flag: "We will serve no group or party but will hew hard to the truth as we find it and the right as we see it. We are dedicated to the whole truth, to human values above all interests, to the rights of man as the foundation of democracy; we will take orders from none but our own conscience, and never will we overlook or misrepresent the truth to serve the interests of the powerful or cater to the ignoble in the human spirit." Of course, it has never paid much.

Contents

Introduction

This book contains no news about the sex life of George W. Bush, nor about the drugs he has ingested, nor about whatever dark psychological demons drive him to seek the presidency of the United States.

No sex, no drugs, no Siggie Freud—so why would anyone read it? For one thing, it's sort of funny. Because it's about Texas politics it's funny—there's nothing we can do about that, and it's not our fault. Numero two-o, the conventional wisdom, which is often wrong, says George W. Bush is the next Leader of the Free World, an arresting concept. The quality of leaders does change history, even in a world supposedly dominated by economic and technological forces. Just for example, Nelson Mandela and Slobodan Milosevic were elected within a few years of one another, each at a point when the unity of his country hung by a hair. They got different results. Since there appears to be a shortage of young Abe Lincolns about these days, it's a mercy America is at no such dire divide.

Young political reporters are always told there are three ways to judge a politician. The first is to look at the record. The second is to look at the record. And third, look at the record.

The method is tried, true, time-tested, and pretty much infallible. In politics, the past is prologue. If a politician is left, right, weak, strong, given to the waffle or the flip-flop, or, as sometimes happens, an able soul who performs well under pressure, all that will be in the record.

So here we are, with a record about property-tax abatement and tort reform, and if that's not a by-God recipe for bestsellerdom, you can cut off our legs and call us Shorty. Can't you see it now, poor ol' Random House touting this book: "Read all about George W. Bush's thrilling adventures with the school-equalization formula, his amazing reversals on the sales tax, and most exciting of all, his tragic failure to take a stand on the matter of 150 versus 200 percent for the CHIP program."

The political career of W. Bush is a fairly funny yarn, on account of being the son of a former president is not . . . how to put this . . . not actually sufficient job training for the governance of a large state. Fortunately, in Texas, this makes no difference.

Unqualified to govern Texas? No problem! The single most common misconception about George W. is that he has been running a large state for the past six years. Texas has what is known in political science circles as "the weak-governor system." You may think this is just a Texas brag, but our weak-governor system is a *lot* weaker than anybody else's.* Although the governor does have the power to call out the militia in case of an Indian uprising, by constitutional arrangement, the governor of Texas is actually the fifth most powerful statewide office: behind lieutenant governor, attorney general, comptroller, and land commissioner but ahead of agriculture commissioner and railroad commissioner. Which is not to say it's a piddly office. For one thing, it's a bully pulpit. Although truly effective governors are rare in Texas history, a few have made deep impressions and major changes. Besides, people think you're important if you're the governor, and in politics, perception rules. Of course Texans still think their attorney general, the state's civil lawyer, has something to do with law enforcement too.

*Efforts to rewrite the Texas constitution have been going on for decades. In 1974, we got as far a constitutional convention, but after six months and $6 million, the members voted down their own efforts. They were hopelessly deadlocked over whether to put an anti-union right-to-work clause, already in state law, into the constitution itself. (Right-to-work, one of the most brilliant misnomers of all time, is a phrase originally coined by a Dallas public relations man in 1948.)

In the '99 session, Senator Bill Ratliff, Republican of Mount Pleasant, introduced a constitutional reform bill. "Our constitution was written in the nineteenth century by people terrified of centralized government," said Ratliff. "As a result, we have created the weakest governor in the fifty states. I believe when the people of Texas vote for a governor, they think they are voting for that candidate's programs and philosophy and platform, but the governor has no real authority to institute those things." The Texas constitution, written in 1876, has now been amended 377 times. Most of the 240 state agency heads are appointed by boards and commissions that are in turn appointed by the governor. Because these appointments carry staggered terms, the panels can be dominated by one governor's appointees long after another governor has been elected. And we sometimes get rogue commissioners who turn against the governor who appointed them but cannot fire them. Ratliff's bill would have given the governor the power to appoint the state land commissioner, the agriculture commissioner, the Railroad Commission (a misnomer—it regulates the oil industry), the state Board of Education, and judges—all currently elected. The bill died in House committee. Bush is on record opposing any change to the system of electing judges or to having the Legislature meet only once every two years for 140 days, both considered by good government groups to be appalling systems.

During Bush's first term, the lieutenant governor was a wily old trout named Bob Bullock. By virtue of the constitution and the Senate rules, plus knowing where all the bodies were buried and outworking everyone else, Bullock was the major player in state government. Dubya got along just fine by doing pretty much what Bullock told him to; Bullock became Dubya's mentor, almost a father-son deal. The day Bullock announced his retirement, Bush stood in the back of the room with tears running down his face. Bullock, after a lifetime in the Democratic Party, endorsed Bush for reelection in 1998. Bullock died in June 1999, to mixed emotions from many. At his funeral, one fatuous commentator said of the rainy weather, "The skies of Texas are weeping because we bury Bob Bullock today." This caused a state senator to inquire sotto voce, "So what did Bullock have on the weather god?"

A political record is a flexible creature, and by custom the pol is permitted to burnish his own and to denigrate his opponent's. The record is often used to fool voters. You say your man was for a certain bill, but was he for it before the amendments or after the amendments? Did the amendments gut the bill or strengthen it? In the case of an executive, you can say your man favors such-and-such a measure, but if he does nothing to help it pass—no phone calls, no face-to-face, no threats, no promises, no pleading about how we really, really need to win this one for the Gipper or the greater good; indeed, if the pol quietly lets it be known that no mourning will ensue in his office should the thing die a premature death—then of what merit is his public statement of support?

It's not easy to find the point at which the acceptable stretcher becomes a flat-out whopper, or when emphasizing the positive goes so far it becomes a hopeless distortion of reality. In Bush's case, largely because of the weakness of his office, the hardest task is to find any footprints at all. He has walked most lightly on the political life of the state. And where one can find his mark on a bill or a policy, it often turns out to have been more strongly shaped by others.

What does emerge from Bush's record is that he has real political skills, and those are not to be despised. Politicians rank so low in the public esteem these days, practically the easiest way to get elected is by claiming you are not a politician. "I'm an undertaker! I know dog about politics! Vote for me!" Bush's résumé in office may be slim, but he has worked in and around campaigns for years, knows a lot about the political side of politics, and is good at it. The extent to which credit for his performance should actually go to Karl Rove, the political consultant known as "Bush's brain," is simply unknowable.

Bush's shrewdest political stroke has been a careful wooing of the Hispanic vote. Texas becomes majority minority (now, there's a phrase) in 2008, meaning that blacks and Chicanos combined will outnumber Anglos, according to the demographers at Texas A&M. So wooing the Hispanic vote may seem like a no-brainer, but as you know, Republicans have not, traditionally, bothered much with people of hue. And as that doofus Pete Wilson proved in California, not all Republican governors are bright enough to see the opportunity there.

Bush's second masterstroke has been to straddle the divide between the Christian right and the economic conservatives in the Republican Party, and that is a doozy of a split. In Texas, the Republican Party is *owned* by the Christian right: the party chair, the vice chairs, and everybody on down. When they won in 1994 they kicked out all the old-guard Texas Republicans, those in the school of George Bush the Elder—somewhat patrician, WASP, faintly elitist or Eastern. On the Christian right, such folks are known sneeringly as "country club Republicans." Republicans don't like to talk about class, but there's clearly a class subtext to their internal fights.

W. Bush is himself a born-again Christian who wants a constitutional amendment outlawing abortion, although he seldom mentions that in front of a general audience. During his father's presidential campaigns, W. Bush was detailed to handle the Christian right, so he has years of experience in working with them. In addition, Rove has positioned him carefully toward the Christian right on a series of nasty but largely symbolic issues in the Texas Legislature.

On the other hand, if Bush were perceived as being a creature of the Christian right, he'd have a hard time in a general election, so the masterful straddle has been keeping a moderate face on the Texas Republican Party while keeping the Christian right happy. Bush's record is actually more to the right on social issues than his image suggests, and that includes some of his more eye-popping appointees to what would be a cabinet if we had a cabinet form of government in Texas, which we don't.

Of Bush's credentials as an economic conservative, there is no question at all—he owes his political life to big corporate money; he's a CEO's wet dream. He carries their water, he's stumpbroke—however you put it, George W. Bush is a wholly owned subsidiary of corporate America. We don't think this is a consequence of political calculation; it is more a consequence of his life experience, political thinking, and party affiliation. We can find no evidence that it has ever occurred to him to question whether it is wise to do what big business wants. He is perfectly comfortable, perfectly at home, doing the bidding of big bidness. These are his friends, and he takes care of his friends—sign of a smart politician. That this matches up nicely with his major campaign contributions is a happy synergy for Governor Bush.

Where Bush is weak is on the governance side of politics. From the record, it appears that he doesn't know much, doesn't do much, and doesn't care much about governing. The exception is a sustained effort on education, with only mixed results. In fact, given his record, it's kind of hard to figure out why he wants a job where he's expected to govern. It's not just that he has no ideas about what to do with government—if you think his daddy had trouble with "the vision thing," wait till you meet this one. For a Republican, not wanting to do much with government is practically a vision in itself. Trouble is, when you aren't particularly interested in the nuts and bolts of governing, you end up with staff-driven policy. When someone comes in to see you about the gory details of home health-care payments or job-training outreach, it's all very well to give a disarming gesture of "I give up," as Bush is wont to do, and announce, "I don't know a thing about it; you'll have to talk to So-and-So on my staff." Delegation is a many-splendored thing for any executive, but it only works if old So-and-So understands the problem himself and has any idea what you expect him to do about it.

To this end, it is helpful if you, the chief executive officer of the political entity, do not, as a regular thing, take a couple of hours off in the middle of the day to work out and play video games. It's a curious thing about Bush, who is an observably competitive and almost hyperactive person, that the word *lazy* is used to describe him. You get no sense of laziness from watching him—if anything, he seems to have a rather short attention span and often seems impatient to move on to the next topic or project, leaving an impression of restless energy. When Bush was once asked what his most serious weakness is, he said it is that he doesn't like to read long books, especially books about policy.* That surprised no one at the state capitol; it is a common guess around the statehouse that Bush doesn't even read *Governing* magazine, which is the bible of state government. He has also said that he hates both meetings and briefings.**

However, as the presidential campaign has geared up, the handlers have been buffing his image madly, and he now sprays interviewers with references to his current reading. But it's like his Spanish: best not to inquire in too much depth. Bush has gotten an enormous amount of mileage out of the fact that he supposedly speaks Spanish, and indeed, he has apparently been working on it, which is to say it's better now than it was in the '94 campaign. His accent is good enough that he can cut radio ads in Spanish. But during public appearances in the Rio Grande Valley, he habitually does the same two or three sentences in Spanish and then they cue the mariachis. Rove often cites a press conference Bush held in Spanish with Mexican reporters as proof that he is fluent in that language: "He held an entire press conference in Spanish." The press conference was so Spanish II it was painful.

In general, Mexicans, a courteous people, are the opposite of the French when it comes to their language. If you try to speak Spanish, no matter how pathetic the effort, Mexi-

*Interview with Tucker Carlson, *Talk* magazine, September 1999.
**Texas Monthly,* June 1999.

cans will beam upon you because they appreciate your effort. But we have yet to find a fluent Spanish speaker who thinks Bush could carry on a conversation of any depth in the language. This is just a minor example of the media's stupefying lack of skepticism in their reporting about Bush.

A hoary truism has it that it's better to be lucky than smart in politics, and Bush is. The argument about whether he ever would have been elected to anything if his name weren't George W. Bush is pointless. His name is Bush. Ann Richards used to say, "He's missin' his Herbert," a gibe that didn't work. That W. Bush has traded on his father's name all his life is observably true. In fact, one could argue that he's never really done anything else. But it's also true he had no choice about being his father's son; short of becoming a monk on Sumbawa, he couldn't avoid it and would have been a perfect fool to throw away the advantage. But Bush has also been lucky in his timing: Laura Bush once said, "If George is good at anything, it's timing." And in politics, timing is everything.

Dave McNeely of the *Austin American-Statesman* recently reminded his readers that when Ann Richards was elected governor in '90:

☆ the state faced a budget shortfall of several billion dollars;
☆ the courts had ordered the state to find a way to fund the public schools fairly, since the old system was grossly inequitable;
☆ the prisons were so crowded, dangerous felons were given early release in order to avoid running afoul of a federal court order on overcrowding;
☆ the Legislature was still involved in a fratricidal bloodbath over redistricting; and

☆ the public was eager to get a state lottery, which required a change in the constitution, possible only by a two-thirds vote in the sorely divided Legislature.

Richards and the Lege (pronounced "Ledge," this is the name by which our remarkable Texas lawmakers are collectively known) dealt with all these issues; they raised taxes to generate an additional $1 billion a year and pared state government down even more through the then-innovative and since much-copied Performance Review Audit. As the Texas economy ginned up along with the rest of the country's, Bush inherited a handy budget surplus that came to $7.6 billion by 1999. That permitted the Lege to both increase spending on the public schools and grant the tax cut Bush was so keen on.

Richards and the Lege also dealt with the school-equalization issue, which has been under litigation for almost thirty years, by passing a new school-finance law called Robin Hood, because it took from the rich districts to give to the poor districts. The concept was so controversial in Texas, she might as well have tried to pass the Communist Manifesto in its entirety. The state also embarked on a prison-building spree that tripled the cells in Stripe City. Richards got the two-thirds vote for the lottery with a one-vote margin. By the time Bush came into office, crime was down, school scores were up, and we had a surplus. The 1991 tax increases will produce an estimated $10.4 billion for this two-year period alone. The lottery has produced $6.9 billion since it began in '92, and—here's the beauty part—Bush, who hates trial lawyers with a passion, also got a gorgeous windfall when the tobacco companies settled with the state of Texas. (It's possible Bush's dislike of lawyers stems from the fact that he was rejected by the University of Texas Law School as a young man; this proves, as we have always suspected, that UT has higher standards than Harvard.*) The state was represented by five killer lawyers working for a contingency fee, and they won $17.3 billion from Big Tobacco, the largest settlement in the history of Earth.** So the trial lawyers Bush loathes get the state $2 billion for this budget cycle alone, which happened to just exactly pay for the tax cut on which Bush is running for president. This guy is not just lucky; if they tried to hang him, the rope would break.

One reason Bush is good at politics is because he's a likeable guy; you'd have to work at it to dislike him. He is far more culturally a Texan than his father, at ease with the kind of locker-room bull, rough language, and physical contact characteristic of Texas politicians. (For some reason, Texas pols are extremely tactile, always slapping one another on the ass or the shoulder, hanging on to one another by the elbow or the armpit, whispering right into one another's ears—damned if we know why.) But Bush also exaggerates his Texanness. In 1992, when he was asked how he differs from his dad, he said, "He attended Greenwich Country Day and I went to San Jacinto High School in Midland." Actually, Dubya, who was born in New Haven, Connecticut, went to San Jacinto Junior High in Midland for one year,

---

*Page Keeton, then dean of the University of Texas Law School, wrote one of the people who had supported Bush's application: "I am sure young Mr. Bush has all the many amiable qualities you describe, and so will find a place at one of many fine institutions around the country. But not at the University of Texas."

**Under a contract with the attorney general's office, the five lawyers funded the three-year suit out of their own pockets, paying hundreds of other lawyers and expert witnesses. Bush and his attorney general, John Cornyn, have challenged the lawyers' contingency fee in what is an increasingly ugly and apparently futile series of legal maneuvers.

moved to Houston, attended an elite private school there, and then, just like his dad, went to the high school at Phillips Academy in Andover, Massachusetts, perhaps the most exclusive prep school in the country. (Not to mention earning his undergraduate degree at Yale and his M.B.A. at Harvard.)

Bush is obviously an extremely competitive man with a macho streak that seems to be touched off by other aggressive males. His relationship with the late political consultant Lee Atwater, himself a notorious hard-ass, was clearly competitive, and in Bush's telling of it, he always comes off as tougher than Atwater. He also seems to have copied Bullock to some extent. Bullock was one of the most genuine tough guys in Texas—the man could be meaner than a skilletful of rattlesnakes (which happens to be the kind of metaphor he often used—he was a master of Texian language, which dotes on metaphor and simile). Bullock was such a black belt in ass-chewing that Senator David Sibley coined the phrase "drive-by ass-chewing" to describe the one you got if you happened to stick your head in his office when he was mad at somebody else. For an upper-class white boy, Bush comes on way too hard-ass—at a guess, to make up for *being* an upper-class white boy. But it's also a common Texas male trait. Somebody should probably be worrying about how all this could affect his handling of future encounters with some Saddam Hussein, but that's beyond the scope of this book. Bush's other noticeable problem is the frat-boy factor. Sometimes he's just a little cocky; sometimes he's plain arrogant and comes off as a callow jerk.*

On the other hand, he can laugh at himself. During his

---

*Bush himself is aware of this tendency. In a May 1994 interview with the *Houston Chronicle*, Bush credited his wife, Laura, with helping him mature. "If I am cocky and brash," he said, "I am less cocky and brash because of Laura."

first gubernatorial campaign, he was on the obligatory dove hunt on opening day of the hunting season (even Ann Richards felt obliged to go out and kill the symbol of peace) when he shot a killdee, a protected species, by mistake. Everybody thought that was pretty funny, and so did George W., who had a good time making fun of himself over it.

Bush was once asked which was the toughest decision he'd ever had to make. One might have guessed the execution of Karla Faye Tucker or fighting his own party for school funding and losing, maybe even putting together the deal to build the Rangers stadium. Nope. He said it was deciding to get married. Laura Bush doesn't look like that tough a choice to us.

If, at the end of this short book, you find W. Bush's political résumé a little light, don't blame us. There's really not much there there. We have been looking for six years.

—Molly Ivins and Lou Dubose
December 1999

SHRUB

Class Act: The Texas National Guard and Running for Congress

I remember Midland like some folks remember Mama.
She was a hard old mother, this Midland.
—Larry L. King

Midland was Yuppieland West.
—George Bush the Elder

Austin is a small town of half a million residents. The old neighborhoods within five miles of the capitol still seem like the backdrop for *The Gay Place,* Billy Lee Brammer's 1961 novel set in a two-company town, where everybody works for state government or the university. Even today, government is so incestuous that no secret is safe for long. So the story of how George W. Bush got into the Texas National Guard at the peak of the Vietnam War, got a direct commission, was assigned one of the last two pilot slots in the state after scoring the absolute numerical minimum (25) on the qualifying test, and flew F-102s in a unit staffed by sons of privilege is not a deep secret.

Bush's version is that a friend whose name he doesn't recall told him of an opening in the Texas Air National Guard. He applied, was accepted within a few days, learned to fly an F-102, and would have gone to Vietnam had his unit been called up—an unlikely prospect given the nature of the unit. At one point, he was granted a transfer to Alabama to work on a political campaign. Bush says there was no discreet call from his father, then a congressman representing Houston. No family friends working on his behalf as far as he knew, or at his request, he says. Despite the waiting list of 100,000 men trying to get into the Guard at that time, and a list of 150 pilot applicants who often had to wait eighteen months to be considered for flight school in the Texas unit, he got in. That's his story, and he's sticking to it.

What actually happened in 1968 is that a close family friend of the Bushes telephoned Ben Barnes, then the speaker of the Texas House and one of the more durable and wily characters in Texas political history. This friend told Barnes that Congressman Bush's son needed a spot in the Texas Air National Guard. Barnes called the general in charge of the Texas Air National Guard, Brigadier General James Rose, and recommended George W. for a pilot position.

Barnes aid Nick Kralj also worked for General Rose. Kralj (pronounced "Crawl") is himself a noted Texcentric, owner of a succession of Austin nightspots, and a man given to carrying a concealed weapon long before Dubya signed the bill that made it legal.

A civil suit, and an interview with a former statewide officeholder, confirmed what had long been common knowledge in Austin. Barnes, Kralj, and another Barnes aide, Robert Spellings, ran an underground railroad that quietly moved the sons of privilege from Selective Service offices into a safe haven in Texas Guard units. The unit that accepted Bush included the son of former Texas senator Lloyd Bentsen, the son of former Texas governor John Connally, and enough rich young men to field a polo league. It also included a few black Guardsmen—several members of the Dallas Cowboys football team. Only Bush, however, was promoted as the Guard's anti-drug poster boy, one of life's little ironies given the difficulty he has had answering the cocaine question all these years later. "George Walker Bush is one member of the younger generation who doesn't get his kicks from pot or hashish or speed," reads a Guard press release of 1970. "Oh, he gets high, all right, but not from narcotics."

What gave the Guard story new legs in September 1999—even though it already had been covered by Texas dailies, *Rolling Stone,* the *Los Angeles Times,* and *The Washington Post*—was a civil lawsuit filed by the former executive director of the Texas State Lottery against the company that ran the lottery for the state lottery commission. He claimed that the company, GTECH, had gotten the lottery commission to fire him, which GTECH denied. The lawsuit had nothing to do with Bush's military record. But Barnes had been the top lobbyist for GTECH, and the plaintiff's lawyers wanted to ask Barnes whether GTECH was allowed to keep its lottery contract because of Barnes' perhaps having done Bush a favor thirty years earlier by getting him into the Guard and then keeping quiet about it. Barnes was scheduled for a deposition by the plaintiff's attorneys shortly after Labor Day. ("The rumor," one political operative said, "is that Barnes might actually tell the truth when he's under oath.") Bush, Barnes, and GTECH all dismissed the suggestion that GTECH would have been allowed to keep its lottery contract because Barnes had sat on the National Guard story. Barnes' lawyers called the claim "fantastical" and "so tenuous that any reasonable person would find it preposterous."

It's a story with more subplots than a Mexican telenovela, but what mattered was that in September Barnes finally was questioned under oath about a topic he had refused to address for decades. Kralj was deposed, and others allegedly involved in Bush's Guard enlistment were prospective witnesses. Everyone except Governor Bush was beginning to talk, or at least mumble, to the press about what happened thirty years ago.

Kralj's testimony was additional confirmation that parents who had the right political connections used the speaker's office to keep their sons out of Vietnam. He and Spellings sometimes passed lists of names from the speaker to the general who directed the Texas Air National Guard. Although Kralj also worked for the general, he said he didn't know whether the general acted on the lists the speaker sent him. In a peculiar case of selective memory, Kralj said he could recall none of the names that were on the list in question, but he remembers that Bush's name was not among the names he couldn't recall.

Spellings told *The Dallas Morning News* (which has no power to subpoena or to put people under oath) that he knew what went on in Barnes' office in 1968 and that no calls were made on Bush's behalf.

A few days before Barnes was scheduled to face deposition, two of his friends told *The Dallas Morning News* that Barnes had told them a prominent Houstonian had made the call in G.W.'s behalf. Sid Adger, who died in 1996, was a Houston businessman and friend of Big George's in the sixties, when the two men belonged to the same clubs and sent their children to the same private schools. Adger's two sons also served in the same unit as George W. Bush. According to the two unnamed friends of Barnes', Adger used his influence with the speaker to get Bush into the Air National Guard.

Once everybody started talking, former president Bush apparently felt the need to go on record somewhat ambiguously. "He's fairly certain—I mean he doesn't remember everything that happened in the 1960s—but he said he and Sid Adger never, ever talked about George W. and the Texas Air National Guard," said a woman in the former president's press office. The candidate himself, confronted by the possibility that a sworn account of what had happened might become part of the public record, moved from foursquare denial to complete waffling. "I have no idea and I don't believe so," Dubya said when asked if Sid Adger had called on his behalf. This is exactly the sort of thing that used to drive Republicans into fits about "Slick Willie" Clinton.

There it is. The closer you got to the courthouse, the closer you got to the truth. The statements by the Bushes, *père et fils,* are masterpieces of plausible deniability. Barnes, who was elected lieutenant governor after he served as speaker, cited legal precedents established by Richard Nixon to claim that executive privilege gives him immunity from having to testify about his dealings with the Texas Guard.

Federal district judge Sam Sparks didn't buy the executive-privilege argument, and Barnes began leaking enough of the story to the press so it wouldn't hit Dubya all at once when the depositions became public. When he was finally deposed, Barnes said he was called by Sid Adger on behalf of George W. Since Adger is dead, the story goes no further. (It should be noted to Big George's credit that he helped at least one young man with a deep moral aversion to the war get conscientious-objector status.) Maybe they're letting a dead

guy take the fall, but it is more likely that this is just another instance of how privilege has worked for W. Bush over
the years, without his thinking there was anything wrong
about it, or even thinking about it at all. In brief, because
George W. Bush was the son of a congressman, the grandson
of a U.S. senator, and a member of the country's most privileged social and economic class, he got an easy out from
Vietnam.

The Vietnam War, as we all know, was in part about
class. It was fought largely by those who couldn't escape
military service through college deferments or enlistment
in the Reserves or the National Guard. In her book *Long
Time Passing: Vietnam and the Haunted Generation,* Myra
MacPherson examined the role class played in that war.
She looked at the particularly privileged group to which
Bush belonged. It was not just at Yale that Dubya was a
third-generation legacy. The pilot's billet in Texas was as
much his patrimony as was his membership in Delta Kappa
Epsilon and Yale's Skull & Bones Society and his place in
the graduating class of '68. MacPherson cites a 1970 report showing that 234 sons of senators and congressmen
came of age after the United States got involved in Vietnam. "Only twenty-eight of that 234," she writes, "were
in Vietnam. Of that group, only nineteen 'saw combat'—
circumstances undescribed. Only one, Maryland Congressman Clarence Long's son, was wounded." That was the
closest any of the 535 members of Congress came to personal grief.

Bush actually made a more noble choice than others who
enjoyed the same access to power. Barry Goldwater, Jr., did
"alternative service" in the House of Representatives, and
MacPherson found six senators' sons who flunked physi-

cals. Among the twenty-eight sons of the United States Congress who actually served in Vietnam was Al Gore, Jr., who "felt an obligation to go to the war he detested so that his father's position would not be compromised," writes MacPherson. Tennessee senator Al Gore, Sr., had openly bucked his conservative Tennessee constituency and opposed the war. His son served six months as an Army journalist at Bien Hoa in 'Nam.

MacPherson also looks at the class that wasn't so fortunate, using an almost forgotten program called Project 100,000 to examine an America that George W. never seems to understand. Project 100,000, "instituted in 1966 and billed as a Great Society program, was a vehicle for channeling poor, mostly Southern and black youths to Vietnam's front lines," writes MacPherson. Robert McNamara promoted it and saw to it that standards were lowered in order to "recruit and 'rehabilitate' 100,000 youths annually who had previously been rejected for failing to meet the armed services mental or physical requirements."

Soldiers who filled the slots in what came to be known derisively as "the Moron Squad" were class-based cannon fodder. "The program sent several hundred thousand men to Vietnam and several thousand to their deaths," MacPherson writes. A 1970 Defense Department study found that 41 percent of the soldiers in the program were black—compared to 12 percent of the Army as a whole. And 40 percent of those in the program were trained for combat, compared with 25 percent of the services in general. A 1969 Defense Department report found Project 100,000 had a killed-in-action ratio almost exactly twice as high as other units'. The Army took recruits with IQs as low as 62. The minimum passing composite score on the armed-forces qualifications test had been 30 out of 100. Project 100,000 took those who scored below 10.

The units served an important political purpose: They kept military manpower high enough so that Presidents Johnson and Nixon did not have to end student deferments or call up the Reserves. Project 100,000 was the flip side of the system that kept George W. stateside: a special accommodation by which society looked the other way while the rules were stretched to suit a particular class.

It is not George W. Bush's fault that he was born into the class the system was designed to protect, or that he used the advantage his family provided him to avoid the war. What is troubling is that he has never put himself in the boots of the young men who were marched to Vietnam as Project 100,000 infantrymen. Bush is so blind to the difficulties of life in the nation's underclass that he often seems callous.

You see it on the campaign trail. At a Baltimore summer program for disadvantaged children, the presidential candidate, who a year earlier sold his interest in a baseball team for $15 million, tells a child that increasing the minimum wage is a bad idea because it could "price workers out of their jobs." You see it in the governor's social-policy agenda, which is loaded with punitive measures intended to move people off welfare into jobs that pay a minimum wage he doesn't want to increase. You see it in his criminal-justice policy, with harsh prison sentences for the class that Robert McNamara once referred to as the "subterranean poor." Here is a son of privilege who is completely comfortable in a society where all the entitlements go to those at the top and those whose misfortune it is to live at the bottom are left with "faith-based charity" and stern lectures about sexual morality.

Bush has spoken in several published interviews of his intense dislike for "intellectual snobs" and the "guilt" he thinks many of his college classmates felt over Vietnam or race or their own privileged position in life. In May 1994, he told the *Texas Monthly,* "What angered me was the way such people at Yale felt so intellectually superior and so righteous. They thought they had all the answers. They thought they could create a government that could solve all our problems for us. These are the ones who felt so guilty that they had been given so many blessings in life—like an Andover or a Yale education—that they felt they should overcompensate by trying to give everyone else in life the same thing."

In Michael Herr's classic Vietnam book *Dispatches* is a description of a collage made by a helicopter gunner named Davies at his house in Saigon. "It included glimpses of burning monks, stacked Viet Cong dead, wounded Marines screaming and weeping, Cardinal Spellman waving from a chopper, Ronald Reagan, his face halved and separated by a stalk of cannabis; pictures of John Lennon peering through wire-rimmed glasses, Mick Jagger, Jimi Hendrix, Dylan, Eldridge Cleaver, Rap Brown; coffins draped with American flags whose stars were replaced by swastikas and dollar signs; odd parts clipped from *Playboy* pictures, newspaper headlines (FARMERS BUTCHER HOGS TO PROTEST PORK PRICE DIP), photo captions (President Jokes with Newsmen), beautiful girls holding flowers, showers of peace symbols; Ky standing at attention and saluting, a small mushroom cloud forming where his genitalia should have been; a map of the western United States with the shape of Vietnam reversed and fitted over California and one large, long figure that began at the bottom with shiny leather boots and rouged knees and ascended in a microskirt, bare breasts, graceful shoulders and a long neck, topped by the burned, blackened face of a dead Vietnamese woman."

The view of the sixties from the Deke House in New Haven seems to have been quite different.

There was one occasion when class and access to power proved to be a liability for George W. Bush. In 1977 Bush moved back to Midland, the West Texas oil town where he had attended elementary school while his father built an oil company.

George Bush the Elder now fondly describes Midland as "Yuppieland West," and for all the Bushes Midland seems to be what it was in the 1950s—a sprawling, monotonous suburb where Friday nights are for football, Saturdays for backyard cookouts, and Sundays for worship at a mainstream Protestant church. In 1969, ten years after the Bushes moved on to Houston, cultural geographer D. W. Meinig described Midland as "the purest example of the 'native white Anglo-Saxon Protestant' culture in Texas." George W. once told a friend he wants to be buried there.

One of Midland's native sons who's not so fond of the place is Larry L. King, who wrote of the Tall City in the pages of *The Texas Observer* in 1964: "Home is Midland, where what passes for skyscrapers rises off the bleached face of the vast and mismade plain. Where the oillionaires and neanderthal Republicans with low, sloping foreheads and angry John Birchers (in full tremble over fluoridation of drinking water and impeaching Earl Warren) play and the skies are not cloudy all day. . . . Yeah, I remember Midland like some folks remember Mama. She was a hard old mother, this Midland. . . . I recall of my halcyon years sandstorms and talking in tongues at foot-stomping Baptist

Youth Crusades for Christ and mowing rich folks' lawns under parboiling sun without being offered a snort of ice water."

In Midland, Bush found a career and domestic life. By his account, the years he spent working off his military obligation at a Houston Air Force base one weekend a month were his "nomadic days." Dubya says he was adrift in Houston until 1973 and spent part of that time working for a youth program organized by former Houston Oilers football player John White. He lived in the fashionable (and wild) Chateau Dijon apartments and dated widely. (Reporters on the Bush drug beat continue to work this territory.) It was during the "nomadic days" that Bush had an oft-reported showdown with his father. Dubya was visiting his parents in Washington when he took his younger brother Marvin out for a late night of drinking, arrived home after running over a neighbor's trash can, and asked his angry father if he wanted "to go mano a mano with me, right here?"

By 1975, when Bush returned to Midland, it was somewhat more genteel than the place Larry L. recalled. A generation of oillionaires had sent their sons and daughters out of West Texas to attend school, and those who returned made the city seem a little less isolated and claustrophobic. But as a lonely officer of the ACLU in Midland recently reported, "Gay people here won't come out of the closet for fear folks will think they're Democrats."

Within a period of six months, Bush, then thirty, married Laura Welch, a librarian and an El Paso native who had grown up in Midland, gone to school in Dallas, and lived on "the quiet side" of the party-prone Chateau Dijon apartments in Houston—all without having previously met Bush until they both returned to Midland. Bush also set up an oil company and filed as a Republican candidate for the congressional seat being vacated by veteran Democrat George Mahon. More than one reporter has observed that Bush's makeover from a party animal into a married businessman seems to suggest a political agenda. The oil company existed only on paper. The young Bushes bought a house in the huge sprawling suburb that extends from downtown Midland to the interstate north of the city. Joe O'Neill, a second-generation Midland oilman and childhood friend of Bush's, tells the story to reporters who file through his O'Neill Properties office in downtown Midland. O'Neill and his wife thought George and Laura Welch—daughter of a Midland home builder—would be a good match, though Laura was quiet and had an aversion to politics. O'Neill brought the couple together at a backyard barbecue in June. By November George and Laura were married and had purchased a home, and George was kicking off his political career.

Bush's friends, who weren't aware he was particularly interested in politics, were startled. He said, "They were a little confused about why I was doing this, but at that time Jimmy Carter was president and he was trying to control natural gas prices, and I felt the United States was headed toward European-style socialism." It may seem to some rather a leap to envision Jimmy Carter as a "European-style socialist," but it is not at all unusual for West Texas oilmen. Take our word for it.

Bush won the primary in a runoff, defeating former Odessa mayor Jim Reese. The Texas Republican Party saw in Reese the opportunity to win an open seat. He was well known in Odessa, had run against Mahon once, and had the support of Republicans in the district. In 1999 Reese told Karen Olsson of *The Texas Observer* that he and Bush had "agreed on most of the issues." That may have been, but Olsson tracked down newspaper accounts in which Reese criticized Bush's father for "his affiliation with the CIA and the internationalist Trilateral Commission." In a campaign that was obviously directed at the "neanderthal Republicans" described by King, Reese sent out a letter warning voters that Bush had "Rockefeller-type Republicans such as Karl Rove to help him run his campaign."

Bush in turn renounced one-world government, denied that Rove was involved in the race, and even offered a backhanded defense of the man who today is his chief campaign strategist. Rove, Bush told the *Midland Reporter-Telegram,* "is a 27-year old guy who works in my Dad's office in Houston. . . . He's had nothing to do with my campaign. I doubt if he even supports Rockefeller."

A third candidate forced Bush and Reese into a runoff, won by Bush. "It was a Midland-Odessa contest. People from Midland will always turn out to vote against somebody from Odessa," said Delwin Jones, the state representative from Lubbock, one hundred miles north of Midland. Odessa is Midland's blue-collar sister city, home to the drillers, roughnecks, and roustabouts who work for the oil-company executives who live in Midland. Reese won the hometown vote in Odessa—and sixteen of the seventeen counties in the district—but Bush carried Midland by 4,427 to 1,287. The big margin in Midland won the election for Bush.

Running against Democrat Kent Hance was not so easy. Reese had served as mayor of Odessa and had challenged Congressman Mahon in the '76 election. Hance had served as a state representative and state senator, taught at Texas Tech, and lived in Lubbock, the largest city in the congressional district. The boundaries of the Senate district Hance represented roughly conformed to those of the congressional district Mahon had represented since 1934. And Hance was smart, folksy, funny—and clever.

Hance also knew his voters. Bush didn't, and ran campaign ads showing him jogging, a practice still considered perverse in most of the towns on the Texas High Plains. He also misread his rural grain-belt constituents when he made the case for the Russian grain embargo, only to learn that West Texas wheat farmers were staunch anti-Communists—but not so staunch that they would not sell grain to a market as big as the Soviet Union. Bush was burdened by his image, that of an Ivy Leaguer who had moved to West Texas because he saw an open congressional seat there. (Bush also padded his military résumé, claiming in a Lubbock newspaper ad that he had served on active duty. No one noticed it at the time, but when a reporter covering the presidential campaign asked Bush's press secretary, Karen Hughes, about it, she, with a straight face, calculated that flight school, added to two weeks per year with the Guard, equaled a tour of active duty. This must have amused regular Air Force pilots, who used to refer to people like Bush as "FANGers," for "F—ing Air National Guard.")

When Bush raised $400,000 to Hance's $175,000, Hance made Bush's money another liability, claiming that much of it came from out of the district. Hance painted Bush as an elite Yankee carpetbagger and reminded voters that while Bush was at prep school in Andover, Massachusetts, and in college at Yale, he himself was attending public school in Dimmit and college at Texas Tech.

In a tactic that has since been honed to perfection by Republican candidates, Hance went negative on the eve of the election. One of his friends and supporters, Lubbock lawyer George Thompson III, did a mass mailing to Lubbock churchgoers. Thompson's "Dear Fellow Christians" letter focused on a "Bush Bash" ad in the Texas Tech student newspaper. The ad promised "free beer" at a Bush political rally. Thompson's letter accused Bush of using his "vast sums of money" to persuade college students to vote for him by offering them free alcohol.

Hance probably had the election won anyway, though the letter may have increased turnout in Lubbock. He won 53 to 47 percent and was not only the last Democrat to represent that West Texas congressional district but also the first Republican. In Congress Hance became a "boll weevil"—one of the conservative Southern Democrats who supported Ronald Reagan's agenda. Hance saw the political future of Texas. He gave the Democratic Party one more try as a candidate for the U.S. Senate seat now held by Phil Gramm. Then he followed Gramm into the Republican Party. There's not a lot of difference between a Texas Tory Democrat like Hance and a Texas Republican like Bush. They had a hard time disagreeing on real issues during their congressional campaign. After Hance ran for a few statewide offices, he settled into the life of an Austin lobbyist. He's still funny. His new party affiliation—and his stake in a waste-disposal company with designs on a private nuclear-waste dump in West Texas—led him to contribute $20,000 to Bush's two gubernatorial campaigns. Hance has also signed on as a Bush Pioneer, committed to raising $100,000 for the presidential campaign. Local handicappers think he hopes for an appointment at the Department of Energy.

After losing a race early in his career, former Alabama governor George Wallace swore he would "never be out-niggered again." Race was not an issue in Midland—where

Friday night at the downtown Wall Street Bar & Grill looks like a casting call for *The Unbearable Whiteness of Being.* It's not exactly correct to say Bush was outclassed by Hance; Bush allowed the class issue to be used against him. He was out-poor-boyed and out-Christianed by Hance. Neither of those tactics has worked against him since.

Life in the Oil Patch:
Bush's Oil-Field Career

I was a pit bull on the pantleg of opportunity.
—George W. Bush

*He could go to New York and talk people into
giving him money. That made him a success.*
—Midland oilman

Out on I-20, a few miles south of the Tall City of Midland,
travelers can "explore the world of oil" at the Petroleum
Museum. There one finds the world's largest collection
of antique oil-field equipment—drilling and work-over der-
ricks, blowout preventers, pump jacks, and heater treaters—
sitting in a field of mesquite looking like they're waiting for
a crew of roughnecks to show up for work. Inside is a huge
Texas-tacky geological chart of the substrata of the Permian
Basin, using multicolored shag carpet to depict the various
formations. There's a gift shop, a cheesy re-creation of a
1920s oil-field boomtown, and a slide show that tells the
story of oil as an energy source, accompanied by a musical
score that shifts into a dark minor key when Arabs and
Africans begin to influence the price and availability of
crude oil.

The center of the museum is the Petroleum Hall of Fame, a large gallery dedicated to the heroes of Permian Basin oil exploration. Hanging from the dark, paneled walls are portraits of the men—and one woman—who opened up the oil fields of West Texas: Fort Worth wildcatter Sid Richardson; William and Tex Moncrief; Raiford Burton, who discovered the largest oil field in nearby Ector County; Erle Halliburton, the Oklahoma engineer who developed the well-cementing process and the Halliburton cement company that bears his name; Will and Hugh Liedtke, the Pennzoil oil barons who cofounded Zapata Oil with their partner George Bush. That's the George Bush who was elected president in 1988. The founder of Zapata Oil would have made the cut even if he'd never been elected president. He made his first million dollars in Midland, founded a company, and discovered a lot of oil. "That generation discovered the oil that paid for the development of the North Slope, which is now financing exploration in Indonesia," said a Midland oilman, complaining that all the big deals were done fifty years ago. The portraits are suspended on hardwood tracks and can be advanced as new members are inducted into the Hall of Fame. There's no need to make room for George W. Bush, who is not destined to be included in the gallery of heroes.

By now the stories of George W. Bush, struggling West Texas oilman, are part of Texas entrepreneurial folklore. Dubya and some of his friends tell the story of the poor boy who started with just a tiny trust fund, and reporters too often repeat it without slowing down to ask questions. After a few years adrift in Houston, young George impulsively drives west to Midland, where he lived as a child. All he has is his 1970 Olds Cutlass, $18,000 remaining from his edu-

cational trust fund, and a resolve to make it on his own—
by bootstrapping his way up from land man to CEO of a
drilling company. Barely slowed down by the loss of a race
for Congress, he ties up some mineral rights, lines up some
investors, and starts drilling. It is 1978, and George W. Bush
is in the by-God West Texas awl bidness.

A bidness, according to one independent oilman who was
betting on the future as the price of West Texas crude rose
from below $15 to $20 per barrel in the summer of '99, that
is easy to understand: "It's the real estate business, with a
revenue stream."

There's one thing to keep in mind as you read the many
stories about George W. in the oil patch. He got the first half
of that equation. Dubya bought up mineral rights and discovered oil. He just never found a revenue stream—unless
you count investors' dollars flowing from New England and
New York into the alkaline West Texas soil.

The governor's oil-field career can be summed up in a single paragraph. George W. arrived in Midland in 1975, set
up a shell company, lost a congressional election in 1978,
restarted building the company he'd put on hold, lost more
than $2 million of other people's money, and left Midland
with $840,000 in his pocket. Not bad for a guy who showed
up with an Olds and $18K. Not good for the investors who
lost $2 million—unless they were speculating in political fu-
tures and cultivating connections with the son of the vice
president of the United States.

In fairness to our governor, who was one of the more ordinary failures ever bailed out of the oil business, it was easy
to fail in Midland in the mid-eighties. In fact, when oil fell
to $9 a barrel over the winter of '85/'86, Midland itself
failed. The Tall City, visible for thirty miles in any direction

because of the office towers that oil built, hunkered down, took its beating, and will never be quite so tall again.

In 1978 Dubya turned his attention to Arbusto Energy (that's "ar-BOOSTo," the Spanish word for "bush," according to George W., although *Cassell's Spanish Dictionary* gives "shrub" as the only translation). The oil company had made Bush look a little less like the carpetbagger caricature Kent Hance made him out to be. And while West Texas congressional elections don't generally influence the stock market, if George W. had defeated Hance and moved on to Washington, stock portfolios in New England and New York would have been fatter. Arbusto found its start-up money in Greenwich, Connecticut, and other Northeastern cities where Uncle Jonathan Bush could open the doors to executive suites. It was investors from Greenwich—and one fat cat doing business in Panama—who took the hit when Bush's West Texas oil business went south.

Russell Reynolds—the sort of investor your average West Texas land man bootstrapping his way up through the oil patch would find a hard sell—was a cold call for Jonathan Bush. "Jon Bush called me one day and told me about his nephew George, who was in the oil business," Reynolds told the right-wing *American Spectator*. "He asked me if I would be interested in investing. So George W. came to see me. And I thought he was an absolute star. A very attractive guy. Being a great friend of the Bushes, I put in a small amount of money in two of the partnerships."

George W. raised a total of $4.7 million in "small amounts," but he has not been too eager to tell the story. What the public knows about Bush's oil-field days has been turned up the hard way: Richard Oppel, Jr., and Charlotte Anne Lucas of *The Dallas Morning News,* Eric Pooley and

Sam Gwynne of *Time*, and David Armstrong of *The Texas Observer* have pored over Securities and Exchange Commission documents to piece together the story of Arbusto Energy, Bush Exploration, Spectrum 7, and finally Harken Oil, the company that provided Dubya his less-than-graceful departure from the oil business.

The money flowed like fresh oil. Prudential Bache Securities CEO George L. Ball invested $100,000. Celanese CEO John D. Macomber and venture-capital investor William H. Draper III put together $172,550. (Both later got political appointments to the Import-Export Bank during the Reagan and Bush administrations.) Lewis Lehrman, a multimillionaire from New York (who was ten years ahead of the checkbook politics of Ross Perot and Steve Forbes—he spent $7 million of his own money to lose a governor's race in New York in 1982), provided $47,500. Fitzgerald Bemiss, a childhood friend of President Bush's and godfather to Dubya's brother Marvin, invested $80,000. "He could go to New York and talk people into giving him money," a Midland oilman said. "That made him a success."

Investors may have had another motive. Most of the money was raised between 1979 and 1982, when George Herbert Walker Bush was either running for president or serving as Ronald Reagan's vice president. And the money came from sources that weren't accessible to your average thirty-two-year-old land man at a start-up company in West Texas. "These were all the Bushes' pals," Russell Reynolds told *The Dallas Morning News* in 1998. "This is the A-Team." (Reynolds helped raise $4 million for President Bush's 1988 campaign and contributed to George W.'s gubernatorial campaigns.) The same A-Team has raised so much money for Dubya's presidential bid that he decided to forgo matching federal funds and the spending caps that come with them. In oil, baseball, or politics, Dubya's M.O. is consistent: leverage the family name and a small investment into really big money, always provided by others.

The A-Team couldn't keep Dubya afloat when the price of oil started to fall. Arbusto had drilled almost one hundred wells, and 50 percent of them hit oil—about average for Permian Basin exploration in the eighties. But all the big, easy discoveries had been made forty years earlier, when President Bush made his first million in Midland. The younger Bush—who on occasion referred to himself as George Bush, Jr., until he began his 1994 gubernatorial campaign—never "bagged the elephant" that would make a profit for his investors. In fact, the best return many investors got was tax deductions; on some projects as much as 86 percent of the capital invested was written off, in schemes so elaborate that one Arbusto prospectus included eleven pages of descriptions of deductions available to investors. President Bush struck oil in the fifties, but at Arbusto in the eighties a tax accountant was more important than a geologist. ("If an Internal Revenue audit of a partnership occurs, there is no assurance that certain deductions allocated to the limited partners will not be challenged," read the pro forma caveat on a prospectus for one Bush limited partnership.)

By 1982, with little more than tax deductions keeping the A-Team in the oil field, Arbusto was badly undercapitalized— almost Ar-busted. Then a white knight appeared, offering to buy 10 percent of the company for $1 million. This was not a steal for Philip Uzielli, considering that the company's book value was $382,376, according to financial statements.

"A company balance sheet can be misleading," Bush

would later say. "There was leaseholds, there was momen-
tum." There was? Even if you don't have a Harvard M.B.A.,
you can run the numbers and place your bets that Uzielli
had not earned his millions in Panama, where he is the
CEO of a company called Executive Resources, on investments like the one he made in Midland. For a million dollars
Uzielli purchased 10 percent of a company worth $382,376—
in other words, he bought assets worth $38,237. Only with
the purchase of an Internet stock in the late nineties could
you buy so little book value for so much money.

Uzielli first officially appears in a 1982 Arbusto SEC
filing, described as the CEO and director of Executive Resources Corporation, Harrow Corporation, and Leigh Products. Mr. Uzielli isn't talking anymore (in fact, since Dubya
locked up most of the Republican money over the summer
of 1999, no one is talking for the record), but it would be
nice to know what he was buying. At the time Uzielli bailed
out his oldest son, George Herbert Walker Bush was vice
president, and a sure bet to run for president. Uzielli was
also a friend of James Baker III, the man who would become
George Bush's secretary of state.

How did Bush and Uzielli get together? The governor says
he never met Uzielli until he stepped forward with $1 mil-
lion to bail out Arbusto. Uzielli told *The Dallas Morning
News* that he met George W. "in 1979, after his father was
director of the C.I.A." Uzielli later said he did not know
George W. at the time of the $1 million bailout. Bush press
secretary Karen Hughes said she does not know when the
two men met. What is known is that this old Princeton
friend of James Baker's dropped a million dollars on a losing
venture owned by the son of the vice president of the United
States. "What Uzi was betting on, he's betting on me. He's

betting on the oil business, he's betting on the ability for the industry to expand," Bush told *The Dallas Morning News* in 1994, when his business dealings were questioned by Democratic governor Ann Richards.

"Uzi"—speaking to the *Morning News* from his father's home in Florence, Italy—called his Arbusto venture a "losing wicket." But, he added, management was not responsible for the company's poor performance. He had invested in a wildcatting deal and lost money, but it was "no fault of George," he said, adding that the "good Lord didn't put any oil there." (In West Texas, there *are* geologists paid to find where the good Lord put the oil.)

Arbusto's next move was clearly George W.'s fault. In the one major business decision he made, in 1982 he changed his company's name to Bush Exploration (at a time when his father was taking office as vice president) and offered shares to the public in order to expand and raise $6 million needed to keep the company working. He only raised $1.4 million. "I really realized that I had made somewhat of a strategic error," he said, in somewhat of an understatement. Investors outside the circle of family friends paid more attention to the bottom line than to the name on the company letterhead.

Ask him today, and Dubya will tell you that his investors made money—and that an American Petroleum Information Corporation report ranking Arbusto 993rd in Texas, with sixteen producing wells at 47,888 barrels per year, "sounds a little low." Read his prospectus and SEC filings. Limited partners contributed $4.67 million to various Bush funds through 1984 but got only $1.55 million back in profit distributions. They did get $3.9 million in tax write-offs. The oil bidness was not good to George W. Bush's investors.

By 1984 Bush (this time, Bush Exploration) was in trouble again. Oil-patch investment sources dried up as the price of oil, which a few years earlier had been climbing like the 1999 Dow Jones Index, no longer seemed a sure bet. OPEC pushed prices to an unprecedented $34 per barrel before the collapse, and West Texas was more focused on the petropolitics of Saudi Arabia's Sheik Yamani than on the price of feeder calves at the Livestock Exchange in Fort Worth. Dubya was yet again bailed out by big money. This time it was Mercer Reynolds III and William O. DeWitt—two big-league guys who would later become major contributors to his father. Like Dubya, DeWitt had a B.A. from Yale and an M.B.A. from Harvard. His father had owned the Cincinnati Reds, and he owned an oil company in need of someone to direct its Texas operation. Instead of hiring a headhunter or placing an ad in *The Wall Street Journal,* he buys a failing company so he can hire its CEO, and George W. Bush becomes the third-largest shareholder in Spectrum 7.

After a good start, Spectrum 7 also began to sink, and neither its recently hired CEO in Midland nor the major-league guys in Cincinnati could keep it afloat. Again, as predictably as the hero would pull the damsel off the railroad tracks in *The Perils of Pauline,* another investor showed up to save Dubya's ass. Harken Energy Corporation, which Richard Behar of *Time* magazine in 1991 called "one of the most mysterious and eccentric outfits ever to drill for oil," stepped in to buy Spectrum 7 *and* George W. Bush—whose father was at the time president of the United States. Harken, run by a New York lawyer and Republican Party funder by the name of Alan Quasha, had been all over the map, buying oil wells, oil companies, and gas stations while selling large blocks of stock to investors such as George

Soros and Harvard's Endowment Fund. Bush was a good acquisition.

Bush, DeWitt, and Mercer got $2 million in stock in exchange for Spectrum 7, which had lost $400,000 in the six months prior to the sale. "The banks hadn't foreclosed," Harken director Stuart Watson told *Time* in 1991, "but that was in the wind." Bush himself received stock worth somewhere around $500,000 and an annual consulting fee of $120,000, later reduced to $50,000. Bush is fondly remembered in Midland for getting on the phone and finding work for all of his company's management and executive employees when he finally cashed in. Again this class distinction: Those who get a golden parachute instead of a pink slip are not culpable. They didn't invent the system.

"We didn't have a fair price for oil, we just had George," a Harken director said later. "And George was very useful to Harken. He could have been more so if he had had funds, but as far as contacts were concerned, he was terrific. . . . It seemed like George, he knew everybody in the U.S. who was worth knowing."

If George didn't know them, they knew him. In 1991, on the eve of the Gulf War, Harken didn't strike oil, but it did strike a big deal: an exclusive thirty-five-year exploration contract with the Persian Gulf emirate of Bahrain. The deal made no sense to anyone in the oil business. Harken was a small Texas company with no international or offshore drilling experience and, until the billionaire Bass family of Fort Worth was brought into the deal, resources nowhere near sufficient to undertake a major exploration-and-drilling program off the coast of Bahrain. "It was a surprise," a senior analyst for Petroconsultants told *Time*. "Harken is traditionally not a company that explores for oil internationally." *Forbes* (the magazine, not the candidate) got the same word from an oil-business analyst in Houston, who called the deal "hard to imagine. A tiny company with no international experience drilling in the Middle East." When reporters asked W. Bush if his financial interest in the region might have influenced his father's foreign policy, he found the idea inconceivable. "No, I don't feel American troops in Saudi Arabia are preserving George Jr.'s drilling prospects," Bush told the Associated Press in 1990. "I think that's a little farfetched." In all likelihood, he was right. But he got testy whenever reporters got close to what might have been driving the deal. Asked whether his involvement with the Dallas energy company lent it added credibility in the Arab world, Bush told *The Wall Street Journal:* "Ask the Bahrainis."

That wasn't necessary. *Journal* reporters Thomas Petzinger, Jr., Peter Truell, and Jill Abramson followed Harken into the White House, where Palestinian-born Chicago investor Talat Othman suddenly showed up on three occasions to discuss Middle East affairs with President Bush. The connection? "Mr. Othman's political access coincides with the remarkable ascendance of a little Texas oil company on whose board he serves alongside George W. Bush, the President's oldest son," the *Journal* reported. Othman was on the board, representing Sheik Abdullah Bakhsh of Saudi Arabia, a 16 percent Harken shareholder. Othman didn't show up for ceremonial coffee in the Map Room, a photo op with the president, or a sleepover in the Lincoln Bedroom; he was invited to the White House with a small group of Arab Americans who were advising the president of the United States. An administration source quoted in the *Journal* said Othman's connection with Dubya and Harken didn't get him a meeting with the president, but Othman had been recommended by "many people in the Arab-American community."

But there is more to the *Journal* story than questions about whether George W. got a business colleague into his father's White House. At the center of its December 6, 1991, story (which, eight years later, has more news value than the daily dispatches from the campaign press bus) is the Bank of Credit and Commerce International. BCCI is long since discredited and dissolved. But when it was up and going, it was a vehicle to convert Middle Eastern oil money into political influence. Sheik Bakhsh, in fact, was a co-investor in Saudi Arabia with Ghaith Pharaon, a fugitive bank exec alleged to have been BCCI's front man in the United States. And Sheik Khalifah bin-Sulman al-Khalifah, Bahrain's prime minister, was one of forty-five investors who owned BCCI Holdings of Luxembourg, the bank's parent company. The *Journal* reported that it found no evidence of wrongdoing or influence peddling by George W. Bush or anyone else connected to Harken. The *Journal* did find, however, numerous links among Harken, Bahrain, and individuals close to BCCI.

The *Journal* observed that "the mosaic of BCCI connections surrounding Harken Energy may prove nothing more than how ubiquitous the rogue bank's ties were." Sheik Bakhsh denied any connection to the bank or that his ties to Pharaon connected him to BCCI. Harken spokespersons bristled when *Journal* reporters asked about their company's relations to BCCI, dismissing the links to BCCI as purely random, and saying they were shocked to learn of them. George W. denied BCCI connections, direct and indirect.

The *Journal* even found indirect social and business ties linking Harken and BCCI. Michael Ameen, the Houston oil consultant who had worked in the Middle East and led the

Bahrainis to Harken, was close to the Pharaon family. For years, the *Journal* found, Ameen had "close-up dealings" with the Saudi royal family and their advisers, including Mr. Kamal Adham, a BCCI principal. Ameen also had served as a State Department consultant, briefing the new U.S. ambassador to Bahrain. The money trail even leads back to Arkansas, where Bush had secured Harken funding from Little Rock's Stephens Inc., one of the largest investment banks outside of Wall Street, controlled by Jackson Stephens (most recently known for his support of Bill Clinton). Dubya had known Stephens as a major ($100,000) soft-money donor to the campaign of President George Bush in 1988. Stephens' wife, Mary Anne, would soon become the Arkansas co-chair of the senior George Bush's presidential campaign. Bush traveled to Little Rock when Harken officials met with Stephens, who connected Harken with Union Bank of Switzerland, which at the time was a joint-venture partner with BCCI in another Geneva bank. Stephens had yet another BCCI connection: In the late seventies he had urged BCCI to take over what was once Washington, D.C.'s, biggest bank company, First American Bankshares.

This is more than just a funny-money story. BCCI was the center of one of the major banking scandals of the 1980s, when an important function of the bank was to use surplus petrodollars to gain access to political leaders. On the eve of an American war over oil in the Middle East, one of the president's regional advisers found his way into the White House through an oil company partly owned by the president's son. BCCI, like Southwestern Bell lobbyists in the Texas Legislature, was everywhere.

In the end, it was a stock sale that created public relations problems for Dubya, which makes sense, because his oil-patch career had more to do with selling investments than drilling for oil. In June 1990 he sold two-thirds of the Harken stock he had acquired in the Spectrum 7 deal at $4 per share—$318,430 more than it was worth when he got it. Two months later, Iraq invaded Kuwait and Harken's stock dropped to $3 a share. It later fell to $2.37.

Bush has repeatedly pointed to the Bahraini deal, saying that he sold "on good news." But as they say in Odessa—Midland's sister city—not hardly. In May, a month before Bush sold his stock, the Harken board appointed Bush and another company director, E. Stuart Watson, to a "fairness committee," to determine how restructuring would affect ordinary shareholders. One "informed source" told *U.S. News & World Report* that Harken's creditors had threatened to foreclose if debt payments were not made, although Harken's treasurer strenuously denied that creditors were poised to seize the company. Smith Barney, Harris Upham & Co., the financial consultants Harken hired, warned Bush and Watson that only drastic action could save the company. Bush took drastic action. He unloaded his Harken stock before news of the company's precarious health was made public, at a time, *U.S. News* wrote, when there was "substantial evidence to suggest that Bush knew Harken was in dire straits." The reason Bush wasn't bothered by phone calls from business reporters inquiring about his stock sale was simple: Insiders liquidating large blocks of stock are required to notify the Securities and Exchange Commission immediately. Bush reported the sale eight months after the federal deadline.

The Wall Street Journal ran a small item about Bush's late filing and said that while the SEC files civil suits against flagrant violators of insider-reporting rules, first-time violators usually get only a warning letter. Bush didn't rob a bank or sack a savings and loan, but his unreported stock sale doesn't pass the smell test, when you consider that the SEC regulation he violated is intended to stop board members from bailing out and leaving less-informed stockholders holding an empty bag—which is exactly what Bush did. Three years later, during his 1994 race against Ann Richards, he claimed he had filed the required report and that the SEC must have misplaced it. SEC spokesman John Heine told *Time* that no one at the agency ever found any lost document.

If Bush does make it to the White House, he and Laura should have Ken Starr over for dinner. If Starr hadn't so abused the power of his office, Congress might have reauthorized the independent-counsel statute, leaving the door open for a court-appointed prosecutor to investigate a president's son who flipped his oil companies faster than a Texas S&L can daisy-chain a Dallas condo; as a corporate board insider, unloaded his company stock shortly before its price plummeted; and walked away from the whole mess with more money than Bill Clinton ever dreamed of making on a little real estate deal now known as Whitewater.

Bush's Harken story ended in 1990. In 2000 none of it matters in Fort Worth, Dallas, or Houston. Texas loves a favorite son. We overlooked the many shortcomings of the late John Connally and cheered when patrician Tory Democrat Lloyd Bentsen reminded Danny Quayle that he was "no John Kennedy." We even came close to getting behind the presidential campaign of Phil Gramm, the political equivalent of kissing a toad. Now everybody loves George W. They love him even more in Midland. Just don't look for his portrait hanging in the Petroleum Hall of Fame anytime soon.

Prestanombre:
Bush and Baseball

I'm all name and no money.
—George W. Bush, 1986

I'm mad.
—Eddie Chiles, 1978

Any Texan who owned an AM car radio in the 1970s re-members Eddie Chiles, the late Fort Worth oil-field million-aire best known for his radio spots, which began with: "I'm Eddie Chiles and I'm mad." Each morning at drive time, Eddie would take on government spending, the Environ-mental Protection Act, the Endangered Species Act, excess regulation of business—all in a thirty-second spot delivered in a Texas snarl that was almost endearing.

Every now and then you can still spot an old pickup truck with an I'M MAD, TOO, EDDIE sticker fading into a rusty bumper.

Eddie's radio spots were pure, ideological public service. Suburban homemakers in Dallas and Katy Freeway com-muters in Houston were unlikely to call with requests for eight hundred barrels of drilling mud or a casing perforation job. So the oil-field service company Chiles owned never got much business out of his mass-market advertising.

But Eddie got our attention. And the right-wing radio spots must have strengthened his friendship with President Bush. By 1989 Chiles was ill and trying to divest himself of some business interests. In particular, he was looking for a buyer who would keep his Texas Rangers baseball franchise in Texas. When the president's son showed up, Chiles was an eager seller.

Chiles had a few prospective buyers. One was William DeWitt, who had bailed Dubya out in Midland, buying one of Bush's failing oil-exploration companies and making him CEO of another. DeWitt's family once owned the Cincinnati Reds, and he had known Bush since the 1984 oil-field deal. By 1989 he was ready to do another deal, using Bush as a front man to buy the Rangers.

But baseball commissioner Peter Ueberroth wanted local ownership and wouldn't approve the DeWitt deal because Bush had so little money to put into it. So Bush did what he'd done in all his past business ventures: He got on the phone and started raising money. Back in Midland, Bush would "take his buddies from Harvard to the oil field and show them around, and before we knew it, they were blowing money our way," one of his former employees told a reporter. Baseball was an easier sell.

Bush has claimed that he put together the deal with Dallas billionaire Richard Rainwater and investor Edward "Rusty" Rose. Ueberroth said Bush initially failed, and that Ueberroth himself had to go to Dallas to sell the project to Rainwater. In the end, Chiles sold and Bush bought. Or at least Bush and what he has called a "bunch of big little guys" bought a baseball team. The bigger "little guys" included:

☆ Dallas billionaire Richard Rainwater, who made his fortune managing the mega-fortune of Fort Worth's multibillionaire Bass brothers

☆ Rusty Rose, a Dallas business associate of Rainwater's known as "the Mortician" because of his uncanny ability to profit on dying companies

☆ Roland Betts, who attended Yale with Bush and worked in New York financing movies (at $3.6 million, Betts was the largest single investor in the team)

☆ Fred Malek, a Washington lobbyist who had worked as President Bush's campaign manager.

There were smaller partners, but "little guys" these were not. For $83 million Bush and seventy investors bought the Texas baseball team that had once been the Washington Senators. Bush paid $640,000 for 2 percent of the franchise, with a clause in his contract that would make that 2 percent 11 percent—if his investors recovered their initial investment. They did, as the Rangers quickly became one of the most profitable sports franchises in the country.

In fact, the Rangers got rich. Not the old-fashioned way, with savvy scouts handicapping prospects at high school and college games across the nation; Bush pushed Ranger scouts to sign Christian athletes, rather than the carousing egos who gave sports a bad name. Johnny Oates, the Rangers' God-fearing manager, is one example of the Christian athletes sought out by Bush. "I got a letter from Governor Bush just the other day," Oates told *The New York Times*, three years after Bush moved from Arlington to Austin. "He'd seen an article about me in the Fellowship of Christian Athletes magazine, and he just said thanks. It's good to know there are believers in positions like governor."

But it wasn't God who made the Rangers rich. The team increased its book value from $83 million to $138 million by convincing the city of Arlington there would be no more baseball unless local taxpayers sprang for a new stadium. Afraid their franchise would find another home, residents of Arlington voted to add a half cent to one of the highest sales taxes in the nation in order to raise the $191 million needed to build the Ballpark at Arlington.

Not satisfied with the taxpayers picking up the tab on the construction of the stadium, the ball team used its quasi-governmental sports authority to "take" the thirteen acres needed for the stadium complex—at a price so low a state court had to step in on behalf of the unwilling "sellers."

Austin journalist Robert Bryce found some contradictions between Bush's business and candidate résumés. In a story published in *The Texas Observer* in 1997, Bryce reported that Bush had campaigned on property rights and in his first legislative session as governor signed into law the state's first property-rights or "takings" legislation. The 1995 law is based upon the "sanctity of private property" and makes it difficult for state and local governments to prevent sprawl, protect urban water supplies, or save critical wildlife habitat. More than difficult—semi-impossible. The law—advanced by the property-rights or "wise use" movement—requires state and local government to compensate landowners when-ever government policy adversely affects private property value. The wise-use movement is one of those odd marriages between big business and the extreme right. Now and again one of its right-wing thinkers goes off script and provides a look inside. Marshall Kuykendall, a leader of the Texas property-rights movement, was asked a few years ago to cite one single example of the government seizing property without just recompense, since the Constitution expressly forbids this. Well, huffed Kuykendall (and he does huff), what about the Emancipation Proclamation, setting slaves free, taking private property with no compensation whatever to their owners from the feds? Kind of hard to think of a response, isn't it? Property-rights law is one of many bad public-policy concepts being field-tested in Texas before being exported to other states.

Bush ran for governor in 1994 as a defender of private property, a position that doesn't entail a lot of risk in Texas. "I understand full well the value of private property and its importance not only in our state but in capitalism in general," Bush told the Texas Association of Business. "And I will do everything I can to defend the power of private property and private property rights when I am the governor of the state."

Three years earlier, when Bush was a managing partner of the Texas Rangers, he had a different notion about "the value of private property" in our state and "capitalism in general." In 1991 the Rangers management pushed a bill through the Legislature, creating the Arlington Sports Facilities Development Authority, whose sole function was to build a stadium for the Rangers. The sports authority was given the legal power of taxation and eminent domain. In effect, this meant that the team could acquire land and raise revenue. As outrageous as a baseball team condemning private property might seem, it is the process by which stadiums are built in most states today, with ball teams and local boosters going to state legislatures to create quasi-governmental sports authorities to do the building and assume the debt while the team collects the revenue.

Socialized sports is not unique to Texas. But the Rangers

did go at it with a certain regional zeal. In fact, the baseball Rangers used the same tactics the Texas Rangers of another era used to drive Texas Mexicanos off the land they rightly owned. The Rangers management went out and made an offer. When landowners refused, the sports authority condemned the property.

It would have been easier if the owners of the thirteen acres that were condemned to build a stadium had been a bunch of working stiffs living in trailer parks in Farmers Branch. But it wasn't a trailer park, it was more like Highland Park, the flossiest suburb in Dallas. The land was owned by the heirs of Texas television magnate Curtis Mathes, and they clung to the quaint notion that they could name the sale price for a piece of property they owned.

The "taking" for the Ballpark at Arlington started a range war that ended up in district court in Fort Worth, a town owned by the billionaire Bass brothers but still home to enough Bubbas to find twelve jurors sympathetic to the little guy. And Bush's baseball club—with its lineup of millionaire and billionaire owners, and the sports authority's right to condemn private property and raise taxes— made the Mathes television millionaires look like Chicano field-workers.

Court documents tell the story of the real estate agent the Rangers hired to approach the Mathes family. "I was not very well received," the agent wrote in his memo to the franchise management.

The sports authority's appraiser assigned the Mathes land a value of $3.16 per square foot, "a total value of $1.515 million." The memo went on: "An offer was made by the Authority at this price. The offer was rejected & the Sellers countered with $2.8 million for all three tracts, i.e.:

$5.31 p.s.f." Unhappy with that price, the authority, which is actually a quasi-governmental front for the ball team, offered the sellers $812,220 for the land. The baseball guys knew how to play hardball. While they were preparing to condemn the property, they wrote another potential buyer, the owners of the Six Flags theme parks, to wave them off. The ball team, after all, had something the theme-park operators didn't: the right to condemn and take land. Six Flags could find its thirteen acres somewhere else.

Bryce even dug up a memo the real estate agent wrote to Rangers president Tom Schieffer, telling him Ms. Mathes was not being cooperative and the city of Arlington would have to condemn her land. How much of a free ride did these corporate land rustlers expect? The same memo urged the Rangers to "get the City to hire qualified, experienced outside condemnation counsel" to start the proceedings to acquire the land for the ballpark.

"What happened to my folks was pretty audacious," the property owners' attorney said after the trial. "It was the first time in Texas history that the power of eminent domain had been used to assist a private organization like a baseball team."

When the jury ordered the sports authority to pay the Mathes heirs $4.2 million as just compensation for the land taken at a lower price, Arlington city manager Bill Studer, who also serves on the sports authority board, told the press that he expected the Rangers to pay. A reporter asked Rangers management if the team would pay any part of the $4.2 million. "Our position is, that is a judgment that's against the sports authority, not against the city or the Rangers," said Tom Schieffer. "The sports authority has to pay that." The authority, lest we start to believe the bureaucratic jargon, is the taxpayers of Arlington, where every cab driver, burger flipper, lawyer, schoolteacher, and bank teller has paid for a few bricks in the pretty Ballpark at Arlington. If *chutzpah* were a word in Texas, one would use it here.

The ball team isn't getting a completely free ride. The stadium will be turned over to the Rangers in 2002, and the Rangers will pay a grand total of $60 million in rent before the city hands them the title to the $191 million stadium. "He's not an entrepreneur," Arlington lawyer and anti-tax activist James Runzheimer said of Bush. "He's a welfare recipient."

Professional baseball was a great fit for Bush. Teams filled with Christian evangelicals, high-stakes deals with other people's money, a kids' game for grown men. He loved all of it. In the summer of 1991 he and two other Ranger owners (including an in-law who had come down from Connecticut) would change into swimsuits and tennis shoes and shag fly balls in the Arlington Stadium, the old minor-league ballpark that served as the Rangers' first home. It's a wonder Bush left baseball to run for a job the speaker of the Texas House says "involves an awful lot of ribbon cuttin' and not enough power."

When Bush was elected governor, he put everything he owned in a blind trust—except his interest in the Rangers. That would have been a change of franchise ownership, he said, and required the approval of the baseball commissioner. In 1998 Governor Bush cashed in, selling his 11 percent interest in the team for $15.4 million.

Hillary Clinton had done a far smaller deal on commodities futures in the 1970s, and the East Coast press stopped just short of appointing its own special prosecutor to look into allegations that she was trading on her influence as the wife of the governor of Arkansas.

Here in the Great State, the son of a sitting president served as what Mexicans call a *prestanombre*—a small player who lends his name to a project run by a big player. Our *prestanombre* got the taxpayers to provide a big chunk of added value to his business, was elected governor, and made a $15 million profit on a $600,000 investment and his family name.

It makes commodities futures look like peanuts.

Campaign '94:
Bush v. Ann Richards

He is governor today because of guns.
—Ann Richards

The 1994 campaign of George W. Bush against Ann Richards is probably not particularly helpful as a predictive tool for the 2000 presidential race because it was in many ways a freak race in a freak political year. But Bush's political style has not changed since then, nor have Karl Rove's political tactics, so there are instructive points to be made. And the first of these is: Don't underestimate George W. Bush.

Labor Day is traditionally the kickoff for political campaigns, or at least for their shift into high gear. Spring primaries may or may not be interesting; in the summer we snooze while the parties try to mobilize their faithful. And then comes September. In statewide polls taken around Labor Day 1994, Ann Richards had approval ratings of well over 60 percent: crime was down, school scores were up, the economy was humming, there were no new taxes, and throughout this favored land the sun was shining bright. Nine weeks later she was out of office.

The simple explanation is God, gays, and guns.

For several years now, Ann Richards has avoided talking about George W. Bush on the sensible grounds that anything she says will be dismissed as sour grapes. But Richards remains one of the shrewdest political observers in Texas, and her autopsy of her own campaign is dispassionate and merciless. She ran a bad campaign. Of Bush, she says, "We didn't underestimate Bush, but we underestimated the Christian right, which probably reached its zenith that year. We underestimated the NRA [National Rifle Association] and its money. That cost me the male union vote, the good ol' boy vote. I lost that over guns. Bush was very firm on the concealed-weapons legislation, that he would sign it. I could not do it, in my conscience I could not cross that line. He is governor today because of guns."

As for the year, 1994 was the year of the Republican Revolution, when Republicans took control of both houses of Congress for the first time since 1952; the year seventy-three Republican freshmen were elected to Congress; the year Newt Gingrich quarterbacked a nationally coordinated campaign and went on to become speaker of the House. The Republican tide was strong everywhere, but it was especially deep in Texas that year. Democrat Jack Brooks of Beaumont, who had been in Congress since the invention of dirt, was defeated by Steve Stockman, a nutter with militia ties. Democratic judges and D.A.'s were wiped out all over the state. Bill Clinton, almost two years into his presidency, had raised taxes with a one-vote margin, admitted gays to the military in his waffly way, and gotten his brains beat out on his health-care proposal. His name was dookey in Texas.

And Ann Richards had vetoed the concealed-weapons bill passed by the Legislature in 1993, which would have made it legal to pack a rod almost anywhere. She said all along she would veto it, but the NRA put up a helluva campaign to convince her to sign it; one of their more innovative tactics was to try to persuade the feminist guv that Texas women would feel ever so much safer if they could only carry guns in their purses. When Richards vetoed the bill, she observed wryly, "You know that I am not a sexist, but there's not a woman in this state who could find a gun in her handbag."

In addition to being pro-choice, an abomination to the Christian right, Richards had, in the course of making more than 2,700 appointments to state boards and commissions, named six people who were openly gay or lesbian. This became the source of an underground campaign, particularly in East Texas, involving rumors of lesbianism and other unspeakable perversions all taking place in that notorious sink of iniquity, Austin. The saying is that Austin is to Texas what Berkeley is to California. Richards' campaign staff made up a joke game that year: You had to put a bumper sticker on your car and drive though East Texas, and whoever made it back to Waco alive won. The bumper sticker was to say: I'M THE QUEER ANN SENT HERE TO TAKE YOUR GUN AWAY. It was that kind of campaign.

The fact is Richards was far more popular with the general public than she was with the "insiders" in Austin. She'd been through two bruising sessions with the Lege, and a lot of the members didn't like her—not because she was female but because she consistently tried to outmacho the macho. And she was known to treat her staff badly. By 1994,

Richards was tired to the point of exhaustion. She had enjoyed the job for perhaps the first two years, but the '93 session was especially brutal. Many of her top aides think she ran again in '94 only out of a sense of obligation to her supporters. (This is a claim Bush has dismissed contemptuously.) She not only had to campaign all day, but she took stacks of work home with her every night. W. Bush is a far easier-going governor and more popular with legislators. Richards can good-ol'-boy as well as anyone in Texas, but Bush is also exceptionally good at the locker-room joshing, slap-on-the-butt stuff, political hoo-ha.

On another level entirely, it was a tough race, and any Texas Democrat can tell you why. Richards won in 1990 in large part because the Republican nominee, Claytie Williams, was as useless as ball moss. As we say in our quaint Texas fashion, it's one thing to step on your dick, but Williams just stood there and stomped on his. He refused to shake Richards' hand when they encountered each other at a do, an ungentlemanly act that riled everyone. Then he threatened to "head her, hoof her, and drag her through the mud." He publicly reminisced about going to Boys Town on the border to "get serviced" in whorehouses. Imagine how well that went over with Tejanos. And then he told the world's oldest rape joke ("Bad weather's like rape; if it's inevitable, just relax and enjoy it"). None of this amused the women of Texas or the more sophisticated "new Texans," who cringe at the state's cowboy image. So in 1990 Richards got both the suburban swing vote and a big chunk of Republican women. But in '94 both went to the other side, with the nonthreatening, affable, well-mannered Bush, who refused to rise to Richards' barbs. That suburban vote keeps growing and growing in Texas as people move here from other states; there are now more votes in Collin and Denton counties, north of Dallas, than there are in the entire Rio Grande Valley. Those two counties alone can wipe out any margin a Democrat picks up from the Tejano vote in the Valley.

Richards' campaign polls showed her with a personal approval rating over 60 percent but with only 47 percent of the vote. And that figure never moved during the entire campaign: Bush kept coming up and she didn't move. Her popularity didn't translate into votes; she was the one the voters said they'd rather have over for dinner, but the swing voters would say, "Well, yeah, I like her, she's done a good job, but let's let him have a turn now." And the motivated voters were all on the other side—Clinton-hating, Christian-right, gay-bashing gun toters—the usual splendid assortment our state offers. Richards, who governed as a moderate, hadn't done much to make environmentalists or minorities get out and work their asses off for her, even though 47 percent of her appointees were women, 20 percent Hispanic, and 14 percent black. (The equivalent figures for Bush after six years are 36 percent women, 13 percent Hispanic, and 9 percent black.)

Some who know the Bush family well believe Dubya ran against Richards at least in part out of a vindictive grudge stemming from her making fun of his daddy. Richards' famous line about Big George—"born with a silver foot in his mouth"—was a zinger for the anthologies, and according to some sources, there are grudge-holding Bushes. President Bush, always gracious, had a silver pin in the shape of a foot made up and presented it to Richards, who was quite fond of wearing it. W. Bush himself says he is more like his mother.

As a candidate, W. was almost fanatically "on-message"—
mostly because he didn't know enough to wing it. Every
time he tried, he got into trouble. Given Richards' record,
there wasn't much to attack except the gun veto, but there
was an anomaly in the crime statistics. While overall crime
had declined by almost 20 percent over four years, juvenile
crime appeared to be on the rise because stats on juvie crime
had only just begun to be kept as a separate category in
Texas. Bush made this into not just an issue but almost
a fetish. You could ask him the time of day, and out would
come the canned response: "We must curb juvenile crime."
His graphic campaign ads showed a grainy, apparently
real-life incident of a helpless female being set upon and
beaten by two masked male muggers. It turned out the shot
was set up by adman Don Sipple and was also used in campaigns in California and Illinois that year. Bush's version
originally claimed, "Crime is out of control." The ad was
later amended to "Juvenile crime is out of control. Ann
Richards is out of touch if she thinks Texans today feel safer
than they did a few years ago." Quite true, they didn't feel
safer; every focus group and poll put crime as the top concern, and violent and gory murders still got top billing on
the news every night. Bush's ads proclaimed, "Crime has become more random, more violent. Incredibly, Ann Richards
says she reduced crime and violence in Texas." Incredible
but true, though one can argue that Richards' building more
prisons is not what reduced the crime rates.

Bush got a nice boost from the case of Michael Blair, the
Willie Horton of the 1994 campaign. Blair, who had served
eighteen months of a ten-year sentence for burglary and in-
decency with a child, was paroled a year before Richards
took office. In March of '94 he kidnapped and murdered a

seven-year-old in Plano. Richards had cut early release of violent offenders by two thirds and tripled the minimum sentence for capital murder. But Bush's ads claimed, "We don't keep violent criminals behind bars." Bush proposed the elimination of parole for rape, child molestation, and murder. He declared, "Crime in Texas is becoming more random, more violent, and the criminals are getting younger than when she took office." He quoted his own ads. He never let up. By the time he got through, citizens had the impression that packs of feral teenagers were roaming the streets. He is as disciplined a candidate as we have ever watched.

They held two debates, and up against Richards, who has as quick a tongue as anyone in politics, Bush held his own. He wasn't brilliant or impressive, but he was on-message and made no mistakes. Richards did her best to gig him, sometimes using condescension: "He's real well intentioned. For what he knows, he is trying to find some way to rise above his previous experience." Rove, no fool, fired back, "We expect the governor to have her snappy, belittling comments when she doesn't have a program." Richards mocked Bush before Democratic audiences: "You can't just look in the mirror one morning and decide, 'I'm so good-lookin', I should run for office.'" Bush replied, "My mission is to keep the debate at a level where we talk about the future of our state, not focus on all kinds of silly stuff and one-liners and try to tear each other apart."

Because Texas is the original low-tax, low-service state, some of Bush's attempts to "git tuff" were pretty funny. This is a favorite thing for Texas pols to do—they like to git tuff on crime, welfare, commies, and other bad stuff. Bush proposed to git tuff on welfare recipients by ending the allowance for each additional child—which in Texas is $38 a month. This led to the mind-boggling vision of some welfare queen producing a new child annually in order to get an additional $38 a month. Bush also tried to make an issue of the Texas Commission on Alcohol and Drug Abuse having hired a recovering alcoholic as its executive director. Ten years earlier, former state representative Ben Bynum of Amarillo, then a county commissioner, had cashed about $2,000 worth of checks—often at liquor stores—drawn from a fund to promote a new courthouse. He got ten years probation, sobered up, and became a substance-abuse counselor. His conviction for misapplication of public funds had been expunged. The Bush campaign put out a release: "Gov. Ann Richards should be forced to explain why she would allow Bynum, a convicted felon, into a position of public trust to oversee millions in taxpayer funds." Bush said, "I wouldn't have appointed him." Two days later, Bush was forced to note, "The governor doesn't appoint the executive director, of course."

In early summer, Rove pulled Bush off the hustings and they all went to East Texas for a weeklong come-to-Jesus session. Bush never got off-message again. Richards took to calling him "the phantom candidate" because he so seldom went into an unscripted situation—television interview, press conference, even one-on-one interviews. Bush said, "I know she's baiting me. She expects me to behave like Claytie Williams by aggravating me into saying something foolish." Richards at one point referred contemptuously to what "some jerk running for office" might say, a remark that hurt only her.

Bush's top political troika was already in place by the '94 campaign. Joe M. Allbaugh served then, as now, as his campaign manager and later his chief of staff. Allbaugh, a huge man physically, both tall and broad, is a longtime political op who had previously served the governor of Oklahoma. He is gifted at both organization and fund-raising, not to mention his outstanding service to major contributors (since a source of contention in the SCI lawsuit: see page 103). Bush's press secretary, Karen Hughes, is tall, smart, energetic, and exceedingly loyal. Also pretty damn tough. She comes from a military family—her daddy was the last governor of the Panama Canal Zone. She is a former television reporter, and it is not at all unusual to find her the last spinmeister left in the press bar after a debate. Texas reporters, long accustomed to her, watch in some amazement as she diligently works the national press pack, memorizing names, making friends, bullying those who trespass against the good name of George W. As though it had never happened to any of us.

But premier among the troika of W. Bush's counselors is Karl Rove, the new Lee Atwater, the Republican James Carville, the man. (Always excepting, of course, the fact that if anyone gives Rove too much credit, it pisses off Bush, who then feels obliged to publicly humiliate Rove. "Is the Rove news conference over?" Bush once growled.)

Rove was reportedly politically conservative from a very young age. He went to high school in Salt Lake City and attended the University of Utah. He has described himself as "a diehard Nixonite." Unlike Bush, Rove was active in student politics. He supported the war in Vietnam and told the *Dallas Observer,* "I was living in a relatively conservative state, and it was hard to sympathize with all those Commies." In the summer of 1971 Rove left college and moved to Washington to become executive director of the national

College Republicans. Two years later he ran for the office
of chairman of the organization; his Southern-states campaign manager was the late Lee Atwater, who later became
something of a legend for running take-no-prisoners campaigns. In 1977 Rove moved to Houston as executive director of a political action committee co-chaired by Bush the
Elder and James A. Baker III, future secretary of state.
Rove's friendship with W. Bush dates from this era. "I was
supposed to give him the keys to the car whenever he came
to town," said Rove.

Rove worked on Bill Clements' first campaign in 1978,
became his chief of staff, and launched his own political consulting firm on the side. He has worked for almost
every Republican statewide officeholder, including Senators Phil Gramm and Kay Bailey Hutchison, Chief Justice
Tom Phillips, and Attorney General John Cornyn. From
1991 to 1996 one of Rove's clients was the Philip Morris tobacco company, which paid him $3,000 a month at a time
when the state was suing the tobacco industry. At Bush's in-
sistence, Rove sold his consulting firm before signing on
with the presidential campaign. Bush wanted Rove's full
attention.

Rove is known as "Bush's brain" in part because he is a
superb campaign tactician. In September 1993 Rove wrote a
memo urging the campaign to "limit GWB's appearance . . .
to reduce the attention of the Capitol press corps." This is
the first known instance of Rove's preference for not letting
Bush loose in any unstructured situations and for keeping
him away from the press. He did the same in 1999, with a
"Rose Garden campaign," announcing that Bush would be
entirely too busy with the state's business during the legislative session to do any presidential campaigning. Bush was

not only being tutored daily for the presidential campaign, but Rove and Allbaugh also arranged for planeloads of contributors to be flown in to have lunch with him almost daily. In public, Bush agonized over how the "possible" presidential campaign would affect his wife and daughters; privately, he was collecting tens of millions of dollars.

Rove is also the source for much of Bush's political philosophy. He not only considers Myron Magnet's book *The Dream and the Nightmare* a towering work (see page 69), but is also behind much of the "values" campaign in which Bush, a rather unlikely source of moral authority, preaches the solid middle-class virtues of thrift, sobriety, and personal responsibility. Rove reinforces Bush's antagonism toward "intellectual snobs" and "intellectual arrogance," which at times slops over into a dislike of anyone who is Eastern. This is a grudge Bush has carried since his college days, when he apparently felt looked down on as a frat rat by more cerebral types. Despite his pedigree and prep school, Bush ran into some Eastern stereotyping of Texans, a common experience for Texans in the East. This was far more prevalent in the days when Lyndon Johnson was regarded as a Visigoth by the Eastern establishment. Bush told the *Texas Monthly*, "There's a West Texas populist streak in me, and it irritates me when these people come out to Midland and look at my friends with just the utmost disdain." This can more or less be made to fit into Magnet's theory that countercultural types are the authors of the moral downfall of the poor. Rove talks to Bush every day by phone, sometimes up to twenty calls a day.

For years Rove was regarded as a junkyard dog of campaign consulting, no holds barred. In one incident, a political opponent of Phil Gramm was forced to return a contribution from a gay group in San Antonio when Rove raised a stink about it. But the '94 campaign allowed Rove to take the high road. Claytie Williams ran mean against Richards in '90, and it was a disaster. So Bush stuck to Rove's chosen issues: juvenile crime, tort reform, and education.

"The Democratic Party's back was broken when Ann went down," said one of the state's top political consultants. One consequence is that Bush has had an amazingly easy ride as governor. While Richards was governor, the veteran Fred Myers chaired the Republican Party and Karen Hughes was its executive director. They put out press releases attacking Richards almost daily and filed open-records requests on state agencies constantly, looking for ammunition. They sued Richards to get her telephone and appointment logs and raised hell about the expenses filed by her appointee to the state's liaison office in Washington. The drumbeat was constant from the beginning, clever exploitation of every political misstep and weakness. Whereas Bush faced no political opposition as governor, the chairman of the state Democratic Party spent all his time desperately trying to get the party out of debt. The Texas press was supine as well, in part because many capitol reporters simply like the outgoing Bush. Another factor, much gossiped about but not written about, is the effect of Bush's presidential ambitions on Texas' capitol press corps.

It was clear to insiders Bush was going for president well before his second gubernatorial campaign, and it also became clear that at least some Austin bureau chiefs had decided to hitch their stars to Bush's wagon. He was their ticket to Washington, their entree into the bigs, their chance to become talking heads on the Sunday chat shows. The result was a genuinely embarrassing amount of ass-kissing by some political reporters.* And some Texas newspapers feel it is their role to support the homeboy in a national race. So Bush's second gubernatorial campaign was a cakewalk, an almost pathetic mismatch: Bush had $20 million; the Democratic nominee, land commissioner Garry Mauro, raised $3.5 million. Bush won 69 percent to Mauro's 31, in a clear display of political muscle-flexing designed to impress Bush's potency for presidential-campaign purposes. Although in what may turn out to be an ominous sign for Bush's presidential chances, in his one debate against Mauro, Bush did not come across well.

The only good to come out of it was when polls showed Mauro picking up points on the issue of putting a nuclear-waste dump in Sierra Blanca, on the border in West Texas. Bush had frequently said he supported that location because it was perfectly safe. But when Mauro began gaining ground on it, Bush changed his stance, saying he would support the site only if scientists confirmed it was safe. This gave Bush's commissioners at the Natural Resources Commission the signal to deny the permit for the dump while leaving Bush still in good smell with the utility companies that wanted it.

Bush did learn from the campaign against Richards. In

---

*This tendency to brown-nose is so pronounced, *The Texas Observer* once opined that if the press corps' noses got any closer to Dubya's behind, reporters would be in violation of the state sodomy laws. Paul Burka of the *Texas Monthly* is one of Bush's most devoted followers in the media. In a personality profile of Bush in the June 1999 issue, Burka wrote, "If, as his detractors have charged, he is a middle-aged frat boy at heart, it should be remembered that the slogan of the French Revolution, the seminal event of the modern era, was 'Liberty! Equality! Fraternity!'—and perhaps what is wrong with American politics right now is that in our battles over liberty and equality we have neglected the commonality that is implicit in fraternity." According to several published accounts of the Deke House at Yale in the mid-sixties, the commonality of man was not its strong suit.

order to prevent any repeat of the Michael Blair/Willie Horton effect, the entire parole system in the Texas Department of Criminal Justice was effectively shut down for over eight months in 1998. One trusty—Robert Hudspeth, who had served his mandatory minimum—was counting on what seemed to be well-earned parole in July—he had the endorsement of the wardens. He was so distraught when parole was denied—as usual, with no given reason—that he walked away from his trusty's job, stole a car, drove to Marble Falls, and hanged himself.

Dubya, Billy Graham, and Mel Gabler: Bush and Religious Belief

Does God Almighty hear the prayers of a Jew?
—Reverend W. A. Criswell on who gets into heaven

Mom, look, all I can tell you is what the New Testament says.
—George W. Bush on who gets into heaven

Get me Billy Graham.
—Barbara Bush on who gets into heaven

Normally, it is not the function of political reporters to poke into a politician's religious beliefs. But Governor Bush has invited such scrutiny, and indeed his private religious beliefs are so much a part of his public political pitch, we would be remiss not to explore them. This is not a candidate running on whether the $200 billion or the $800 billion tax cut would be better, or if car-pollution standards should be tightened. If you're looking for one easy way to distinguish compassionate conservatism from pragmatic idealism (Al Gore's equally vapid slogan), religion is it.

In late May 1999, Bush's probable Democratic rival, Al Gore, sat down for a forty-five-minute interview with seven religion reporters from major publications. *The New York Times'* religion writer reported afterward, "To hear the name Merleau-Ponty trip off the tongue of a major American

politician is surely extraordinary." Seemed that way to us—
we never heard of him. Gore also touched on Reinhold
Niebuhr, Teilhard de Chardin, and Edmund Husserl during
his discussion of faith. According to the *Times'* Peter Stein-
fels, Gore's faith is of "a personal Christianity that is ethical
and intellectual, but not especially doctrinal." Gore actually
has some formal religious training. As a young man, he returned from his tour as an Army journalist in Bien Hoa and
went to divinity school for a year. After his tour with the Air
National Guard, Bush spent a lot of time in the bars of
Houston.

Bush also discussed religion with a *New York Times*
reporter. Sam Howe Verhovek, then the *Times'* Texas corres-
pondent, led his Sunday-magazine profile of the overwhelm-
ing favorite to be the next president with the following
anecdote:

> George Walker Bush was visiting his parents in the White
> House one day when the talk turned to religion. . . .
> "Mother and I were arguing—not arguing, having a
> discussion—and discussing who goes to Heaven. . . ." Bush
> pointed to the Bible: only Christians had a place in heaven.
> "I said, Mom, look, all I can tell you is what the New Tes-
> tament says. And she said, well, surely, God will accept oth-
> ers. And I said, Mom, here's what the New Testament says.
> And she said, O.K., and she picks up the phone and calls
> Billy Graham. She says to the White House operator, Get
> me Billy Graham.
> "I said, Mother, what are you doing?"

Bush told Verhovek that Graham, when called upon to
referee this theological dispute, told them he agrees with
George W. "from a personal perspective," but then he gently

admonished both mother and son: "I want to caution you both. Don't play God. Who are you two to be God?"

What we have here is not so much a religious discussion as a political damage-control operation. Ever since his 1994 race against Ann Richards, the story has followed Bush that he believes only Christians are granted God's grace. The story first appeared in a profile by Patti Kilday Hart for *Texas Monthly.* At the time, the leading religious figure in the state was the Reverend W. A. Criswell of the First Baptist Church of Dallas, the world's largest church. Criswell had publicly asked: "Does God Almighty hear the prayers of a Jew?" And he had equally publicly answered with a firm "No." (Reverend Criswell often spoke on behalf of the Lord.)

So here's Bush, five years later, trying to fix the deal. Verhovek reports Bush was "chuckling at the memory" of being upbraided by Billy Graham. And why not? This homely vignette suggests humor and humility, and he is using the Sunday supplement of the nation's most prominent newspaper to redefine his position on who gets into heaven—saved by the *Times.*

Bush has repeatedly told the story of his personal salvation. (For those not familiar with evangelical Christianity, the critical—indeed the only—question is: "Have you accepted Jesus Christ as your personal savior?") In the summer of 1985 W. Bush went to "summer,"* as per longstanding custom, with his parents in Kennebunkport, Maine. While there, he met with the Reverend Billy Graham, who asked him if he was "right with God." W. Bush replied that he wasn't sure, and began to think about it.

*Real Texans do not use the word *summer* as a verb.

A year later, W., Laura, and several friends went to the Broadmoor Hotel, a grand old Western resort in Colorado Springs, to celebrate his fortieth birthday. He woke up with a hangover, but it wasn't serious enough to keep him from his daily jog—a matter on which he is also devout. After the jog, he quit drinking cold turkey, went back to Midland, and got involved in Bible-study groups at First United Methodist Church, where, he has told interviewers, he began to enjoy singing hymns and attending ice cream socials with his daughters. (The daughters are a pair of charming twins who have thus far managed to lead normal lives in and out of the confines of the governor's mansion—first at exclusive private schools in Dallas and Austin, and recently at an Austin public high school.)

Since the Christian right became a political power, conversion testimonials have become common fodder. By the 1988 Republican National Convention in Houston, Elizabeth Dole appeared before two thousand delegates at Pat Robertson's prayer breakfast to share her salvation story, and no one blinked an eye. Dubya has taken his testimonial on the road and tells of his conversion experience—but only before selected audiences.

Dubya's use of his religion for political purposes—our only concern with it—gives him a good leg up with evangelical voters. Poor Mrs. Dole is stuck with the story of her rise from perfunctory churchgoing—with "God neatly compartmentalized, crammed into a crowded file drawer of my life, somewhere between gardening and government." W. Bush has a far more dramatic tale—saved from a life of sin, drinking, womanizing (before marriage), and, by inference, drugs—all of which comes under the rubric "indiscretions of my youth." It's not clear what went on in the valley of despair from which the governor was saved, but we know he was saved. He retails this story in niche markets around Texas, telling it for evangelical audiences only. Hannah Rosin of *The Washington Post* was an early observer of this phenomenon. She noted that candidates adopt "familiar rhythms of religious confession, telling narratives of their own salvation in Christ—substituting, in essence, an evangelical style for a substantive stand."

The trouble with doing this kind of thing in Texas is our state has more je ne sais quoi than normal places, and that includes our preachers. So here's the governor all tied up with James Robison, a Fort Worth televangelist. Bush appeared on Robison's *Life Today* television ministry and invited Robison to be the main speaker at the prayer breakfast in Austin on the day of Bush's second inauguration as governor.

The story Robison told at the prayer breakfast—a familiar one to his followers—centers on rape and abortion. As he tells it, "A little lady walked into a hospital forty-six years ago" in response to a newspaper ad soliciting someone to "take home a little baby boy." Robison then reveals that the baby boy in question was himself, that his birth mother was raped, and had *Roe* v. *Wade* then been the law of the land, "I would not be standing before you today, preaching the Gospel." He says he has gone on to adopt the children of other rape victims who somehow escaped the state's abortion clinics. He incorporates into this sermon the lachrymose tale of sitting with his momma—"the lady who walked into the hospital and saved my life"—on the day she died, saying, "Thank yuh, Momma, thank yuh." Robison is a master of the vibrato. So that was the kickoff for the 1999 session of the Texas Legislature.

This association has raised eyebrows. Bud Kennedy, a columnist for the *Fort Worth Star-Telegram,* asked, "Why would a Methodist governor wander into the televangelist's domain, where stern sermons are spliced between money requests and crackpot Y2K warnings?"

Bush, like President Clinton and other pols, regularly appears in church pulpits, picking up the pace around election time. But the distance between, say, First Baptist Church in Houston—where he spoke the night before he announced his presidential committee—and Reverend Robison's studio is a lot more than the 250 miles between Houston and Fort Worth.

As former President Bush once said of Al Gore, Robison is "way out there, man." He often chats with God on the freeway between Arlington and Dallas: "God said, 'James, you're praying with a greater maturity now.' I said, 'I don't understand, Lord.' He said, 'You're like so many others.' " And so forth.

Robison's greatest claim to fame is that he brought T. Cullen Davis to Jesus. Davis, once a Fort Worth multimillionaire, is sort of the O. J. Simpson of Texas. Two decades ago Davis was tried on charges of shooting his about-to-become-ex-wife, Priscilla, killing her boyfriend and her twelve-year-old daughter, and plugging a few others. It was a pip of a trial, with the Johnnie Cochran role played by Racehorse Haynes, one of the state's showier criminal-defense lawyers. Haynes got the case moved to Amarillo, where he persuaded a jury that Davis was not "the man in black" wearing the stocking mask who entered the mansion that night, despite the fact that Priscilla and two other witnesses identified Davis as the perp. Davis was later tried yet again for allegedly hiring a hit man to knock off the witnesses who had testified against him, and was again acquitted. After Robison helped T. Cullen find Jesus, Davis held a huge party at the mansion, with good eats, Japanese lanterns lighting the grounds, and a sound system announcing over and over, "The son of Stinky Davis has found the Son of God."

Robison persuaded T. Cullen to sell ol' Stinky's art collection and donate the proceeds to his ministry. This plan was being put into effect when Robison had a revelation that Stinky's collection of carved jade and ivory from the Far East was not, in fact, art, but rather graven images of false idols. So the two of them took it back to the mansion and smashed it to pieces in the driveway with a sledgehammer.

In the spirit of FYI, you may be interested to learn that Davis has since remarried but come down on his financial luck. He now sells Pro-Tec, a skin-care lotion that "may" stop skin cancer. He has since been involved in a peculiar flapette of some note in our national life. In 1994 Yale professor Barry O'Neill became curious about the spread of a list that purported to compare the worst problems faced by the public schools in the 1940s and the worst problems facing them today. O'Neill wrote about what he found in an article published in *The New York Times Magazine* and the *Seattle Post-Intelligencer*. According to the list, in the forties the problems were:

1. talking
2. chewing gum
3. making noise
4. running in the halls
5. getting out of turn in line
6. wearing improper clothing
7. not putting paper in wastebaskets.

Forty years later the top problems had become:

1. drug abuse
2. alcohol abuse
3. pregnancy
4. suicide
5. rape
6. robbery
7. assault.

This list had great currency, particularly among right-wing talk-show hosts, television preachers, and the usual bloviators and scolds ever ready to deplore our manners and morals. O'Neill found that the list was first published nationally by George Will in his *Newsweek* column in January 1987 and picked up a month later by Bernard Goldberg of CBS in a piece on youth and crime. Bill Bennett cited the list while out flogging a book, and Rush Limbaugh then attributed the list to Bennett in his own 1993 book on our moral decay. The Heritage Foundation published it anew, and on it went in a sort of intellectual daisy chain. "Senators, mayors, state education officials, university professors and deans" all cited it, reported O'Neill.

The list was in fact concocted by T. Cullen Davis in 1982, as he followed Robison into a crusade against sex education and in favor of the teaching of creationism. Davis' purpose was to convince those who doubted that American schools are sunk in secular depravity. O'Neill found that Davis had lifted the list of modern offenses from a questionnaire asking principals whether they had reported certain crimes in their schools. The indefatigable O'Neill concluded that the 1940s list is simply urban myth.

———

Back on the Robison front: Bush reportedly prays on the telephone with Robison, though we could get no count of how often. When the Reverend James Dobson of Focus on the Family attacked Bush for his "double-talk" on abortion, Robison came to Bush's defense, arguing that Dobson and other ministers should not try to be "kingmakers." Although Dobson's publishing, radio, and TV empire is far larger than Robison's, it is still politically useful for the governor to have a bona fide televangelist so firmly in his camp. At the inaugural prayer breakfast, Robison, his voice quavering with emotion, declared, "I love George Bush." Should Bush become president, we look forward to Reverend Robison's appearances in Washington, D.C.

As for Bush's political philosophy, as much as it can be discerned, it consists of ideas taken from two writers: Marvin Olasky and Myron Magnet. Their work provides much of what Bush calls compassionate conservatism, which we think is a biblical and ideological justification for further dismantling what remains of the social-welfare safety net.

Olasky is a University of Texas journalism professor and a pilgrim who has progressed from Judaism to Marxism to fundamentalist Christianity. He is best known as the writer who sold Newt Gingrich on the idea that orphanages would be a swell place to rear the children of welfare mothers. *Texas Observer* editor Michael King described Olasky's *Renewing American Compassion* as a guide to applied compassionate conservatism "filled with anecdotes of small-scale Christian charity projects . . . and concluding with pietistic suggestions for readers to engage in compassionate conservatism." ("Teach rich and poor what the Bible has to say about wealth and poverty. Help a poor person negotiate

the legal system. Employ a jobless person. Lead a neighborhood association in a poor part of town. Start a crisis pregnancy center. Give a pregnant teenager a room in your
home. House a homeless person. Adopt a child.") King described Olasky's editorial columns, published in the *Austin
American-Statesman,* as "knee-jerk conservative positions
on the news of the day: welfare is bad, abortions are evil,
affirmative action is racist, public education is hopeless,
the Bible is the final moral authority, and Bill Clinton is the
national nexus of all evil." Olasky is a walk-the-walk Christian who heads a biracial adopted family, for years lived in a
black neighborhood, and in general follows the advice he
gives. A nice man. David Brooks, a senior editor of the conservative *Weekly Standard,* lacerated poor Olasky in *The
New York Times Book Review.* "Olasky's historical judgments are so crude and pinched that one suspects his main
effect will be to buttress the stereotypes of those who are
prejudiced against religious conservatives," wrote Brooks.
He also complained that Olasky has failed to establish "a
sophisticated public theology." Because of Olasky's bibli-
cism and his nostalgia for nineteenth-century almshouses,
he comes across as a sort of dipshit guru.

One of the weirdest things about Olasky's ideas is that we
have already tried them here in the National Laboratory for
Bad Government, but Governor Bush, who is not interested
in policy, doesn't remember it. Another case of bad ideas
that never die. Thirty years ago in Texas we privatized a lot
of welfare functions and handed them out to faith-based
outfits. Our particular specialty was private and religious
homes for wayward children. There was, in fact, a quaint
Dickensian industry, particularly common in East Texas: All
manner of persons set up "homes" for delinquent youth.

Delinquents from other states were regularly consigned to these private homes, which advertised that they could re-form delinquents. Reformatories in places like Illinois were overcrowded, so their officials saved money by shipping the little darlings to be cared for in Texas for a per diem fee. (In Texas we pronounce that "purr dime.")

Many innovative instructional techniques were brought to bear on the wayward children, such as putting them in cages, dousing them with ice water, and making them scrub themselves with wire brushes. In November 1972 a fourteen-year-old girl at Artesia Hall, a school in Liberty County, was forced to swallow lye and left without medical care for three days. That probably would have reformed her, if she hadn't died instead.

In the ensuing investigation of these private homes, the state came across a couple of them run by the late Reverend Lester Roloff, a radio preacher from Corpus Christi. Roloff believed you could beat the Devil out of delinquents and Christ into them; he did not hold with sparing the rod. He also had some unusual ideas about nutrition—based, he said, on the Bible—such as, that a slice of watermelon was an adequate lunch. The state's efforts to shut down Roloff's homes for not meeting state licensing requirements became a pitched battle. Our then–attorney general, John Luke Hill, provoked so much ire from fundamentalists for prosecuting Roloff it probably cost him the governorship in 1978.

The Reverend W. N. Otwell of Fort Worth was another faith-based purveyor of reform for wayward youth. His church was fined $14,500 by Jim Mattox, a later attorney general, for failure to get a license for his boys' home. Otwell said Mattox was ungodly, a tyrant, a homosexual, a Communist, and a wicked man who did not love God. Of course, Otwell called everyone who didn't agree with him a Communist, homosexual God-hater, so it wasn't much of an honor. Besides, Mattox was a full-blooded Southern Baptist. Bush should remember Otwell, who sent some of his godly youth to the state Republican convention in 1988 to protest Bush himself. The state party had refused to allow the Log Cabin Republicans, a gay group, to set up a booth at the convention. Bush publicly disagreed with the party's action. So when the gay Republicans held a protest outside the convention, Otwell's followers showed up to protest the protestors. They carried signs that said GOD HATES FAGS.

A more recent attempt at faith-based public-health policy bewildered legislators. Dr. William "Reyn" Archer, Bush's appointee as state health commissioner (and son of Houston congressman Bill Archer), decided to cut funding for health clinics in the public schools. Archer believes that many diseases are caused by alienation and lack of social cohesion. So he shifted money that might have funded school clinics into studies of the root cause of "diseases of lifestyle." This pleased the Christian right, whose leaders have always believed these clinics are nothing more than Planned Parenthood franchises in the public schools. But it worried some legislators. Archer posted $76,000 job openings for assistant commissioners requiring "knowledge or the ability to comprehend and articulate the conflicting dynamics of love and alienation as root causes of social dysfunction and marginal health status. Knowledge of community ethos relating to dysfunctions and spirituality of human nature." Archer, who is known as "Dr. Love," defended his spiritual approach to medicine and told the appropriations committee that low immunization rates in Houston might be cultural. "It's a fascinating discussion," said Representative Kyle

Janek, a Republican and medical doctor who serves on the appropriations committee. "Because every time I want to talk about love and alienation, everybody wants to talk about polio. Dr. Archer, if I can keep you on point here, I'd like you to tell me what the lack of immunization has to do with love and alienation."

You get some very strange results when you use faith-based programs in Texas, you really do.

On the secular front, Bush's ideas come in part from *The Dream and the Nightmare: The Sixties Legacy to the Underclass* by Myron Magnet, a neoconservative with the Manhattan Institute. Karl Rove loves this book, keeps dozens of copies in his office and gives them out like candy. Although the book seems not to have been much reviewed or discussed outside neocon circles (it was plugged by Mona Charen, Hilton Kramer, Irving Kristol, George Will, Tom Wolfe, and Peggy Noonan), you may have heard echoes of it in early '95 when a triumphant Newt Gingrich vowed to extirpate all traces of the Great Society and "the sixties legacy of permissiveness." It was part of the right-wing vogue of the day to blame liberals for poverty. This may be confusing to some, since liberals are, by and large, against poverty, but according to Myron Magnet's argument, it is precisely their fuzzy-headed anti-poverty programs that are responsible for the chaos of the inner cities. He sees ghettos and barrios as a consequence of liberals having fomented a psychology of victimization among poor Americans that has cut into their desire to bootstrap their way out of this mess. And he further posits that a sixties legacy of "If it feels good, do it" has so afflicted poor folks as to lead them to sexual promiscuity, drug abuse, family breakup, and so forth. Magnet also considers Charles Murray, author of *Losing Ground,* a brilliant scholar. Frankly, in our opinion, Murray is a pseudo-scientific racist. It's tempting to make fun of Magnet's book: If Norman Mailer is responsible for the crack epidemic and Ken Kesey caused homelessness by romanticizing mental illness, can UFOs be far behind? But what you have here is justification for doing away with government programs to alleviate poverty on the grounds that they're bad for the poor, who would be so much better off left to the tender mercies of Christian charity.

Magnet suffers from the suffocating provincialism that seems to afflict all the New York neocons. Don't those people ever get out of Manhattan? Perhaps the most troubling aspect of this silly book is its resurrection of the Undeserving Poor. Poor folk, in Magnet's telling of it, are such a moral mess it would be a waste of sympathy to help them. In our experience, perhaps heavily influenced by our own years below poverty level, the Undeserving Poor are no more numerous than the Undeserving Rich. The worrisome thing about this vastly silly book is that Bush is not a man who reads much, and he dislikes reading about policy. (He does like Kinky Friedman's books, but the Kinkster is a little weak on policy himself.) People who have read only one book can be quite dangerous—witness Timothy McVeigh and all those poor citizens who read Ayn Rand and are struck like Saul of Tarsus on the road to Damascus. Had Bush also read, say, Oscar Lewis, Kenneth Clark, Robert Coles, Michael Harrington, Jonathan Kozol, William Julius Williams, Frances Piven, Nicholas Lemann, or a host of others who are not necessarily bleeding hearts, one would be less inclined to alarm over the impact of this one book.

Compassionate Conservatism: Bush and the Christian Right

The Republican Party is not a church.
—Dolly Madison McKenna at the 1994 Republican state convention

Most of all, I believe in the Heavenly Father.
I am a Texas, God-fearing lady.
—Gayle West at the 1994 Republican state convention

George W. Bush was brought to Jesus by Billy Graham in 1985, but he got religion in the political sense at the state party convention in 1994, when the Christian right took over the Texas Republican Party. To that point, profiles of Bush do not emphasize, or in some cases even mention, his religious orientation. The '94 convention was a high-water mark for the Christian activists who had ridden the Pat Robertson tide through the 1988 state and national conventions. The struggle between the Christian right and country club conservatives had become increasingly acrimonious. At Senate-district conventions, particularly in Houston, a remarkable level of vituperation was achieved by both sides. The Christian right kept gaining and gaining in Texas, finally taking over completely in '94. Among the saddest victims of the shift was Fred Meyer, an amiable Dallas CEO

and friend of Big George's who had dedicated his life to the
Texas Republican Party.

To the Christian right, Meyer represented all the secular, economic conservatives who were insufficiently committed to the constitutional rights of the unborn. At precinct,
county, and district conventions Christian-right activists
kept showing up and taking over—and when they won they
took no prisoners. After a lifetime of Republican service,
Meyer had become party chair six years earlier. During that
time the R's came close to a majority in the state Senate. In
the House, Democrats were lining up to switch parties. But
the Christian right accused Meyer of never having been to
a pro-life rally, their litmus test for party officers. He announced his resignation.

The Christian-right candidate who replaced him was former Reagan White House functionary Tom Pauken, an
abrasive and occasionally mean-spirited but slightly populist Catholic from Dallas. The secular Republicans put up a
bona fide conservative in Texas congressman Joe Barton,
who was endorsed by gubernatorial candidate Bush, Senator Phil Gramm, and Representative Henry Hyde, leader of
the pro-life faction in Congress. Normally, getting the nod
from the party's leaders would be tantamount to election,
but the self-styled revolutionaries of the Christian right
had 70 percent of the delegates in Fort Worth. Hyde wrote
an open letter to the convention, noting that Congressman Barton had taken the defense of the unborn all the
way to China, when he tried to intervene on behalf of a
Chinese woman compelled by law to abort her second
child. Gramm told the delegates he was "pro-life and pro-
Joe" and declared Barton a True Conservative. Barton even
had the support of the state's leading anti-abortion lobbyist,

who spread the word that he had never seen Tom Pauken at a pro-life rally in Dallas. None of it did any good; the Christian right just rolled over Barton. Pauken won with 64 percent of the vote and no floor fight.

The Republicans had much more than just a new chairman. The whole party was born again in Fort Worth. Susan Weddington, a San Antonio anti-abortion and anti-gay activist who was elected vice chair, began her campaign speech by reassuring delegates she is no kin to Sarah Weddington. That Weddington is the Austin attorney who successfully argued *Roe v. Wade* before the Supreme Court. Susan introduced her parents, thanked her mother for bringing her into the world, and told the convention that, had Sarah Weddington grown up in the *right* Weddington family, she would have learned to respect the sanctity of life.

Weddington's opponent for party office, incumbent vice chair Gayle West, told the convention: "I have always stood for the strong pro-life platform of the Republican Party of Texas. Most of all, I believe in the Heavenly Father. I am a Texas, God-fearing lady." She also told them she and her husband attended services *and* Sunday school at Pasadena Baptist Church, and that her thirteen-year-old son couldn't make the convention because he was attending Bible classes. To an outsider, this Christian-off seemed an even contest, but it turned out Gayle West couldn't prove she had ever attended an anti-abortion rally, so she lost.

Delegates prayed in the aisles at that convention, prayed in the Grand Old Prayer Meeting, and even witnessed to reporters in the press pit. Open bars in hospitality rooms— a venerable tradition at Texas political conventions—were converted into gourmet ice cream sundae bars, where chefs whipped up high-cholesterol, custom-order desserts. (This actually slowed news-gathering considerably. You can sip four or five glasses of bad Chardonnay while making your way through half a dozen hospitality suites, but four or five hot-fudge sundaes with whipped cream and walnuts is a challenge. An Austin reporter spread the word that the Supreme Court justices had hooch in their hospitality suite. And a party flak who had once been a *Houston Post* reporter set up a neutral "Christian-free corner," complete with a Swiss flag and warning signs, in the terrace bar at the swanky Worthington Hotel in downtown Fort Worth.)

Dolly Madison McKenna is a card-carrying, country club Republican from Houston who always looks as though she just caught the train down from Greenwich. She ran for party chair as a protest candidate against the Christian right, and even served mixed drinks at her suite. She claimed the paper parasols in the drink glasses represented the Republican "big tent"—Lee Atwater's metaphor for a party tolerant enough to include a pro-choice faction. McKenna's campaign for the chairmanship got off to a rocky start when she quoted the late Senator Margaret Chase Smith of Maine to the press: "The Republican Party has been taken over by the Four Horsemen of Calumny: fear, ignorance, bigotry and smear." McKenna herself warned of "a broad-based agenda that aims to eliminate public education, the Federal Reserve and the IRS by the year 2000." That's pretty much verbatim the platform of the Christian Renewal movement. McKenna also compared "the gay-bashing and intolerance" of the Christian right to the work of neo-Nazis in Europe. When at last she stood before the delegates to speak, she said, "The Republican Party is not a church, and it is not a country club." Her campaign and her speech were then over. The delegates didn't just boo, they roared, stopping her entirely, and then swarmed into the aisles chanting, "We are the party! We are the party!" In case the point needed driving home, the convention chose not to pass a routine resolution honoring their nominee, Bush, or their senator, Kay Bailey Hutchison, on the grounds that their Christian-right credentials were suspect. The Republican Party of Texas had come to Jesus.

For Bush, it was a total immersion, in the Texas Baptist tradition. The Christian right threw out his father's choice for party chairman and replaced him with Tom Pauken, who despises the tepid economic conservatism of Dubya and Poppy.

Bush's speech to the convention was standard Republican fare: more jails, longer sentences, less government regulation, fewer lawsuits, less welfare, and—because this is Texas—more executions. It would have been the perfect speech at most Republican gatherings, but not for this crowd. But no matter, they were driven into his arms by Ann Richards. Richards was their Bill Clinton: irreverent, anti-gun, pro-choice, pro–affirmative action, sometimes profane. She was even dy-vorced. And she was a star. So to 70 percent of the delegates in Fort Worth, Richards was as close to Satan as any sixty-plus, teetotaling Methodist grandmother and former junior high school teacher from Waco can be.

What made Bush acceptable to the Christian right was the smell of victory—he had a name that could raise the money to beat her, and he would put a complete Christian family in the governor's mansion—even though he didn't mention the constitutional rights of the unborn, phonics, or creation science in his speech.

George W. Bush was not Phi Beta Kappa at Yale, but he

understands: You got to dance with them what brung you.
He has learned to dance with the Christian right. It has been
interesting and amusing to watch the process. Interesting because it's sometimes hard to tell who's leading and who's
following; amusing because when a scion of Old Yankee
money gets together with a televangelist who suffers from
too much Elvis, the result is swell entertainment. Dubya's
skillful handling of the Christian right—giving them just
enough to keep them in line—is probably his most impressive political credential. But one must ultimately conclude
that the Christian right didn't get a dance—they got taken
for a ride.

To take the latest chapter first, consider the great school-
voucher debate that never happened in the 1999 legislative
session. Next to constitutional rights for the unborn, what
the Christian right in Texas wants more than anything is
its own schools, untainted by secular humanism and paid
for with tax dollars. The leader behind this notion in our
state is Dr. James Leininger, a big-rich San Antonian who
made his fortune in hospital beds. He is our very own
Richard Mellon Scaife. (Scaife is the Pittsburgh millionaire
who underwrites right-wing journalism and think tanks.)
Leininger first invested millions of his personal wealth in a
broad tort reform movement that has made it very difficult
for injured or wronged individuals to sue business or corporate interests. In the cause of tort reform, Leininger invested
so heavily in so many legislative races, thus electing so many
members, that he pretty much has his own caucus in the
Lege. Not Republican, not Democrat, but "here courtesy of
Leininger." School vouchers are the number-one priority of
the Christian right in Texas and, after tort reform, Leininger's greatest passion. He funds a private voucher program

in the Edgewood school district in San Antonio—the same district that spent twenty-five years in court and finally forced the state to equalize school spending between the rich and the poor districts. Edgewood is a district so poor that the schools had few books, leaky roofs, no chalk, and no toilet paper. Leininger is part of a group of political contributors, including "Son of Sam" Walton of the Wal-Mart family from Bentonville, Arkansas, who seem to be willing to spend whatever it takes to get a voucher program here. Investing out-of-state money in Texas gets a proven return, as the state is quite likely to try whatever right-wing nostrum is fashionable. Walton contributed $500,000 to pro-voucher candidates in Texas. Leininger provided $1.5 million in loans and contributions for the Republican candidate for lieutenant governor, Rick Perry—enough to buy the razor-thin margin by which Perry defeated his Democratic opponent. Of course, Perry was also helped by the fact that he has seriously good hair. Leininger also provided a huge loan for Republican comptroller candidate Carole Keeton Rylander in the last days of the campaign; he gave or loaned a total of $3.8 million in '98, including $65,000 to Bush. Bucks like that, he should have gotten at least a voucher bill in the Senate, with its Republican majority.

At the start of the '99 session, it looked as though Leininger would get his payback. Perry, who presides over the Senate, flogged a bill offered by the chair of the Senate Public Education Committee. Bush proposed a voucher program in his State of the State address, and the Leininger lobby and his Texas Public Policy Foundation began to work the two bodies. Then Bush disappeared. He didn't leave town—he was just busy being home-schooled as a presidential candidate. Former secretary of state George

Shultz, the academic Condoleeza Rice, the economist Herb Stein, and even Carl Bildt, a former prime minister of Sweden, were all brought in to tutor Dubya, trying to get him ready for prime time. While the foreign-policy experts explained to him that the people of Greece are not called "Grecians," Senate Democrats were bottling up the voucher bill.

An unlikely pair of legislators blocked the bill most of the session. The late Greg Luna was a Hispanic Democrat from San Antonio who spent the '99 session in the hospital recovering first from surgery and then from a long series of complications. One of the many peculiarities of the Texas Senate is its lack of a calendar; one "dummy bill" is filed at the beginning of the session and all other legislation is then brought up "out of order" by a two-thirds vote to suspend the rules. The good Greg Luna devoted his political career to public education, and this session he was one of the votes—ten Democrats and two Republicans—providing the margin needed to keep the voucher bill off the floor. Luna wrote Lieutenant Governor Perry asking for a twenty-four-hour warning before any motion to suspend the rules in order to vote on a voucher program. He needed the time to hire an ambulance and a nurse to make the ninety-mile trip to Austin in case one of the two Republicans started to flake. But when the motion was finally made, Luna was too ill to travel. A most unlikely savior emerged. Drew Nixon is a Republican from East Texas who has the singular distinction of being the member of the Lege most recently sentenced to jail; in 1997 he was busted in Austin for soliciting a prostitute who turned out to be an undercover cop. "Do you know who I am?" the senator asked the Austin officer, at just about the time she found an unlicensed gun in his car and busted him for that too. She was somewhat annoyed that he had requested a full-service deal for a discount price.

So there was Nixon, sentenced to six months in a halfway house, which he worked off a weekend at a time. He made the obligatory postconviction public plea for forgiveness, with his wife at his side, and went for counseling. This remarkable player rose to the occasion late in the session; he told Bush that vouchers are bad public policy and that he would not step aside to let the bill on the floor. Bush had arrived to lean on Senator Nixon personally as the press watched. The man who had raised $20 million for one statewide race, been reelected with 61 percent of the vote, and by this time was widely believed to be the forty-fifth president of the United States had to turn one vote from a member of his own party who is, frankly, a dipshit. Bush couldn't do it.

"Aw, he just told me that vouchers were good for the state of Texas, that was all," said Nixon, despite the fact that sources on the Senate floor said he was royally reamed by Bush. Sam Smoot, director of the Texas Freedom Network (a group founded by Ann Richards' daughter Cecile to counter the influence of the Christian right), believes Bush didn't want the bill to come out. "If he did, he would have fought for one. But that would have meant taking a risk and using some political capital." Smoot spent the session lobbying against vouchers and saw no evidence that Bush had done anything until he showed up to lean on Nixon. "Bush takes small steps and leverages them into a lot of support from the Christian right. He throws them just enough meat to appease them, which can be dangerous because they are a constituency that has traditionally been unappeasable." Another reason Bush put so little effort into passing vouchers is because Paul Sadler, chair of the House Education Committee, told him at the beginning of the session there was no way in hell that bill would ever make it out of his committee. But Smoot's reading of Bush's handling of the Christian right is also backed by the rest of his record that session.

Bush supported a bill requiring that a parent be notified before a minor can get an abortion—not a high-risk stand in Texas. He refused to take a position on the hate-crimes bill while his surrogates in the Senate killed it because it provided protection for gays and lesbians. He supported a bill to make it illegal for gays or lesbians to adopt children or serve as foster parents. A particularly nasty feature of that bill was its failure to protect people who had adopted a child in the past and since come out as gay or lesbian; the state could take the child back. Bush could have opposed at least that provision, on grounds of not breaking up existing families. Instead he delivered a little homily about traditional two-parent families.

This man of Andover, Yale, and Harvard also supports the phonics method of teaching, one of the Christian right's odder crusades. It is not mentioned in the Bible but is touted by the Christian right as a sort of universal cure for everything from the decline in reading skills to mass killings at Columbine High. (Actually, the Christian right is not mistaken—phonics is an excellent way to teach reading. But as any good teacher will tell you, not all children learn in the same way, and for some kids other methods work better. In Arizona, where their Lege passed phonics-only, some of the best teachers have already quit.)

Bush attended the pre-session meeting of Leininger's Public Policy Forum and happily associated himself with the Christian right's legislative agenda. The governor's press office failed to inform the media that he would be speaking at this right-wing gabfest. This is also part of the Bush/Rove pattern with the Christian right: treating it as though it were a girl he dates but doesn't want to be seen with in public. He took the exceptional step of signing an amicus brief, with his attorney general, in a case before a federal appeals court concerning the right of student athletes to pray in public. He has also hired Ralph Reed, former head of the Christian Coalition, as a campaign consultant.

Perhaps his oddest kowtow to the Christian right has been what might be called his other voluntary emissions-reduction program—this one aimed at adolescent males. Bush had the state hire the Medical Institute of Sexual Health, yet another of the ubiquitous Dr. Leininger's organizations, to set up a "Governor's Conference on Right Choices for Youth." This was an all-day talkathon in Austin making the case for teen celibacy. An interesting development in fundamentalist theology holds that a young person who has lost his or her virginity can, by dint of earnest repentance and subsequent abstinence, regain something known as "secondary virginity." It's a concept. Speakers at the conference told the assembled educators that birth control allows girls to "sign up for the sexual revolution" and that "somewhere between Woodstock and disco, our generation sowed the seeds to cultural disaster." The program also featured a former member of an inner-city black gang who has found a new life expounding on secondary virginity. And of course no such affair would be complete without an appearance by Bill Bennett, the beefy, avuncular virtue czar. (Texas often produces odd cultural combinations. Here's one you may find amusing: In his days at the University of Texas, Bill Bennett once dated Janis Joplin.) In his keynote speech, Bush, the Secondary Virgin in Chief, warned the audience about the "Pandora's box" of sex, drinking, and drug use.

The whole conference may have been a misstep in the careful Bush/Rove handling of the Christian right. By then the national media pack was dogging Bush's every step, and his appearance raised the hypocrisy issue to such an extent it was reminiscent of Gary Hart's challenge, "Follow me," a sort of dare. On the other hand, part of the Rove positioning campaign is to have Bush speak so often about his "youthful indiscretions" that when they are revealed they will already seem old news.

Bennett said, "Young and male, some of us in college, some of us in high school, did things we're not particularly happy about or proud of later, including myself. That doesn't concern the American people." Bush has made it clear that when it comes to youthful indiscretions, he belongs to the Henry Hyde school of aging: He was a youth until he was forty. Bush told the teachers and administrators at this remarkable chastity rally that what matters is not what we did but what we say—a novel concept—and that we must teach young people that "the rewards of abstinence far outweigh the risks of sex." All of this earned Bush the endorsement of Pat Robertson, a man who had opposed Bush's father, that secular conservative.

In the end, the Christian right gets more sermons than blood, sweat, or policy out of Bush. He talks the talk but rarely walks the walk—and still gets the support of the Christian right. Among other things, it's very shrewd politics. Although Gary Bauer and Dr. James Dobson have figured out his strategy—feed the lions just enough meat to stop them from attacking—it is, as Sam Smoot says, a dangerous game. These disciplined political Christian soldiers have spent the last ten years taking over the machinery of the Republican Party, precinct, county, and state. Now they want a ring, not just a promise. That's one reason Bush and Rove accelerated the nominating process, collecting over $50 million and most of the party's major endorsements before the end of the summer of '99. By that time, Pat Buchanan's attacks on Bush's failure to make an antiabortion stance a litmus test for judicial nominees and Dobson's attacks on Bush's double-talk on right-to-life were already too late. And, as we have seen in Texas for six years, the Christian right will settle for the talk instead of the walk in order to be with a winner. In fact, Bush is willing to cut these folks off at the knees if they get in his way. When Republican Party chair Tom Pauken openly criticized the tax increases in the 1997 tax-reform package, Bush and Rove cut off the party's funding. Pauken won the battle—we lost the tax-reform package as Pauken led the Shiite Republicans to reject Bush's finest effort as governor. The Bush/Rove revenge was swift and effective; they cut off the party's money by directing most of the big contributions into a separate political fund controlled by Bush and Rove. When Pauken announced for attorney general, they backed his opponent, John Cornyn, an almost painfully country club Republican. Word went out to Republican donors that the governor would be most offended if Pauken received their support. So Pauken, the true man of the people in the Texas Republican Party, went down in flames. Pauken had led the Christian right to control of the party—but the country clubbers still have the money, so many of Texas' Christian-right activists are now giving their uneasy support to Bush. Hey, everybody likes to be with a winner. Pauken, however improbably, is now practicing conflict-resolution law in Dallas, and has not endorsed George Bush.

Capitol Crimes:
Bush and the Lege

*This was supposed to be our year. We've been
waiting for this [surplus] since Ann was governor.*
—President of a Texas public university

Not a word about higher education?
—House Higher Education chair Irma Rangel,
after Bush's 1999 State of the State address

You don't need a Ph.D. from the LBJ School of Public
Policy to understand how the Texas Legislature works. Just
walk up Congress Avenue to the capitol, where 150 representatives, 31 senators, and the lieutenant governor—each
for an annual salary of $7,200—meet for 140 days every
two years. Look up toward the second floor. On your right
is the Senate and the suite of the lieutenant governor. On
your left is the House and the suite of the speaker. Straight
ahead is the lobby, where in 1997 1,662 registered lobbyists
representing 2,034 clients earned $210 million. The lobby is
the center of gravity in the Texas Lege. It always ensures
that the business of business is taken care of.

From the speaker's office you can see the white, Greek-
revival governor's mansion across the street. One of the
speaker's perks is a small apartment above his office, so for

the past six years Democratic speaker Pete Laney has been George Bush's neighbor. While Laney doesn't consider himself the governor's adversary, he was the single player in the Legislature to whom Bush had to sell his legislative program.

The current lieutenant governor, who presides over a Republican Senate majority, rode Bush's coattails—and a $500,000 contribution and a $1 million loan from a Christian-right medical-bed magnate from San Antonio— to a narrow win in 1998. His Democratic predecessor, the late and legendary Bob Bullock, endorsed Bush when he ran as an incumbent against Democratic underdog Garry Mauro in 1998. Bullock, who turned against Ann Richards, making her single term as governor grindingly difficult, also shared Democratic Party polling with Bush in 1994.

"I've got a House to run," Laney said when asked about his position on Bush's presidential race. Laney has served in that House since 1972, knows the Legislature, understands political power, and believes in government. He is the last of the statewide Democratic powers and has qualities many of his Democratic predecessors lacked: intelligence and integrity. (Over thirty years, four of our past five speakers, all Democrats, have been indicted for one thing or another— not often convicted, but still indicted. Actually, there is one speaker in there who was not indicted: He was shot to death by his wife, and she was not indicted.)

Laney is as Texan as George Bush the Elder is Old Yankee. A cotton farmer and used-car dealer from the Panhandle town of Hale Center (population: 2,098), Laney presides over the House in a West Texas whine that requires translators for out-of-state reporters. ("Whill the jillmun nyeel?" Translation: "Will the gentleman yield?")

The governor first got crossways with the speaker two months before the January start of the 1997 legislative session. In what was obviously the beginning of his presidential campaign, Bush decided to take $1 billion out of a state budget surplus and use it for property-tax relief. The giveback was included in Bush's tax-reform package, an attempt to lower property taxes by, among other things, increasing one of the highest sales taxes in the nation. The speaker got the news about the $1 billion Bush planned to return to taxpayers at the same time the capitol press corps did, in a faxed press release. "He hit the ceiling," said one of Laney's aides.

Two years later, in an interview in his capitol office, there was not even a suggestion that Laney had ever been angry at Bush. He said it took courage for Bush to take on tax reform—and with a wry smile added that he didn't resent the governor's decision to seize a billion dollars from the budget surplus without consulting the Democratic leadership. "I just appointed a committee to make sure it was done right," Laney said. The committee included the chairs of each of four of the most powerful committees in the House and was given a mandate to examine every aspect of the governor's tax-reform plan, especially its effect on public education.

After one hundred days of testimony and three hundred witnesses, Laney's committee produced a bill that made Bush's lopsided tax-reform package into something far more equitable than the governor had ever intended. Democrats, who are sometimes suckers for good public policy, got it passed as Republicans bolted. And three weeks later the business lobby killed it in the Senate. As we report more fully in another chapter (see page 122), what began as a bold attempt to reform the state's system of taxation ended as a small step in the direction of reform. The governor could claim that he got a billion dollars in property-tax relief. In fact, most homeowners saw little tax relief on their tax statements, because school districts promptly adjusted their local tax rates upward to make up for the lost tax revenue. That disappearing billion is included in the largest tax cut in Texas history, described on the Bush Presidential Campaign website.

In fairness to the governor, the $3,000 raise for public-school teachers might not have passed two years later if Bush hadn't begun the school-finance discussion in 1997. But the 1997 tax rebate paved the way for his 1999 giveaway of $1.7 billion in surplus funds—in a state that is yet to fund kindergarten in all of its public schools.

The governor recommended no appropriation for the state's Rainy Day Fund, so it got none. State budget wonks consider it dangerously underfunded at $81 million, and it would have been a prudent budget choice for a conservative governor with $7.6 billion in surplus funds at his disposal.

Higher ed got no additional funding, although the state system is suffering growing pains. "This was supposed to be our year," said a university president. "We've been waiting for this [surplus] since Ann was governor."

Laney describes Bush as a well-intentioned governor who is committed to good public policy, when he is not too influenced by the advisers running his presidential campaign. The speaker might be too generous, considering that he has occasionally given his committee chairs discreet orders to stop certain legislative packages pushed by the governor— such as the second round of tort-reform bills Bush pushed for in '97. Laney has also put out the word that any school-voucher bill would have a hard time in the House, no matter what Bush wanted. During the 1999 legislative session,

Laney reportedly called in Bush's chief legislative aide to tell him he had overstepped his limits in the House.

If you want some idea of what sort of policy President George W. Bush might pursue, the House is a good place to look. Consensus *über alles* rules the Texas Senate, where backroom deals hide many of the real fights over public policy. But in the People's Chamber, the governor's agenda is out there for everyone to see. What has he fought for?

In 1995, two years before tax reform, there was tort reform. And it didn't require the governor to make much of a fight. Tort reform—insulating corporate interests from lawsuits filed by consumers, workers, injured parties, and the survivors of those killed through malice or negligence—has been at the top of the big-business agenda since the 1980s. (President George Bush regularly railed against "trial lawyers in tasseled loafers.") In 1987 the state's chambers of commerce, the Texas Chemical Council, the home builders' lobby, hospitals, HMOs, doctors, and pharmaceutical companies set out to create a level playing field in the state's court system. In this case, that tired sports metaphor meant a judicial system that allows corporate defendants to write the rule book and hire the refs.

When the tort reformers of the late eighties failed, they poured millions into election campaigns and by 1994 eliminated the Democratic senators who had stood in their way. In the Texas Senate, bills only get to the floor when twenty-one senators vote to bring them up, so eleven senators can block any bill. In 1994, after years of being outspent at the polls, the beleaguered Texas Trial Lawyers Association lost its eleven-senator defensive line and the playing field belonged to the business lobby.

Dubya, who ran on the issue in '94, declared tort reform a "legislative emergency," putting all tort-reform bills on a fast track. It was good legislative politics, ensuring that opponents of tort reform couldn't tie up the bills until late in the session. It was good electoral politics, encouraging business funders to give generously, in a state where there are no limits on campaign contributions. And it cut into the income of plaintiffs' lawyers, a major source of campaign contributions for Democrats.

Texas juries used to have a reputation for being friendly to injured parties suing bidness. But no more. Plaintiffs now have to sue corporations in their hometowns. Punitive damages that once reached deep enough into the pockets of companies to alter their bad behavior—for example, the exploding gas tank on Ford's Pinto was repaired under the pain of punitive damages—are now capped. Juries in wrongful-death cases now calculate that a wealthy person's life is worth far more than a working stiff's. And beyond legislation, the tort reformers poured money into the Texas Supreme Court elections, purged the court of Democrats, and have bought and paid for the most anti-consumer, anti-worker high court in the nation.

Asked to respond to a *New York Times* story that found plaintiffs had little success after tort reform, Bush said the old system "was bad for business and bad for the economy in Texas." Pressed about the rights of workers and consumers, he said, "Government should create an environment that encourages entrepreneurs to create wealth." That "good-for-bidness" litmus test is Dubya's real measure of the value of public policy. The *Times* found the lower insurance rates—promised by tort reformers to consumers once those outrageous lawsuits were out of the way—never materialized, even though insurance-company profits are way up.

In 1997 Bush promoted another scheme that was good

for bidness and provided him a great campaign one-liner: *I privatized welfare.* Bush's initial welfare proposal in the '94 campaign was to drastically reduce the rolls by cutting families off after two years and forcing them to go to work. This time his staff decided the "Privatization Study" section in the state's 1995 welfare-reform law was a license to hand over the state's entire welfare certification-and-distribution system to a corporation not previously noted for its interest in the poor: Lockheed Martin. IBM and Ross Perot's old company, EDS, were also in the hunt for the $2- to $3-billion contract, but when Bush aide Dan Shelley resigned and went to work for Lockheed, the smart money was on the defense contractor.

If nothing else, handing the state's welfare system over to a defense contractor would give a certain clever redundancy to the term "corporate welfare." But there was one hitch: The state needed a waiver from the federal government. When the feds were slow to respond, Bush started talking Texan to the Clinton administration, leaning on Health and Human Services secretary Donna Shalala to approve the waiver. In a two-paragraph letter he told Shalala: "You promised an answer last Monday. In my state, we take people at their word." He also warned White House chief of staff Erskine Bowles that "indecision is not in the best interest of our taxpayers or the welfare recipients we are trying to help. Please do us a favor and decide."

The Clinton administration almost bought it. "The White House didn't seem to understand the political implications," said Garnet Coleman, the Houston state rep who finally convinced the Clinton administration that turning a state agency over to a defense contractor that could increase its profits by decreasing enrollment was bad policy and bad politics. Coleman got a hand from AFL-CIO national president John Sweeney, who understood that a corporation in the welfare bidness could increase profits by firing the state employees administering the welfare programs, then rehiring them at half the wages with far fewer benefits.

The governor lost, but in 1999 was back with a welfare-reform package that had more to do with New Hampshire and Iowa than with Texas. Before the session began, his staff met with the Center for Public Policy Priorities, a think tank originally funded by a group of Benedictine nuns (some Austin lobbyists affectionately refer to them as "the twisted sisters"). Patrick Bresette, a policy analyst at the center, said the Bush team patiently listened to arcane recommendations about innovative use of Temporary Assistance to Needy Family funds, additional funding for child care for children whose parents had moved from welfare to work, and job training. "When the session began," Bresette said, "all they were interested in was the punitive one-liners."

"The governor wanted a welfare bill that was full of draconian sanctions," said Elliott Naishtat, chairman of the House Human Services Committee. "They wanted permanent disqualification for felony drug convictions, for fraud on applications or failure to report occasional sources of income, and for noncompliance on child support, like a woman's failure to disclose the name of a child's father. And they wanted full-family sanctions," which would cut benefits to the children of mothers who fail to show up for work training.

All welfare reform had to move through the committee chaired by Naishtat (the only member of the Texas Lege with a New York City accent). So he found himself caught between urban Democrats who wanted support for welfare recipients moving into jobs and a governor who wanted tough sanctions. Naishtat's committee staff met with Bush's staff and negotiated some of the draconian measures out of the bill, still concluding with what Naishtat calls "a very conservative welfare-reform bill." He was later told the compromise that had been agreed to was not acceptable. "It would go upstairs to the political office and come back to us with what they called a few technical changes," Naishtat said. The "technical changes" that followed several negotiated agreements were always the reinstatement of the same draconian measures the House found unacceptable.

One afternoon Naishtat was walking some out-of-town visitors out of the capitol. "Someone steps up behind me, and all of a sudden I'm in a bear hug. And it's George Bush, and he says to me, 'Elliott, I understand we are having some problems with the welfare bill. You're going to give us something we can work with, right? I'm counting on you.' "

The capitol-steps wrestling match, with Naishtat jokingly calling out to nearby state troopers for help, was not unusual for one of the most amiable, up-close-and-personal governors this state has ever known. Midway into his first legislative session, all but 6 of the 150 state representatives and 31 senators had either met with Bush personally or had dinner at the governor's mansion. And with Bush it's not just first names, it's nicknames: Representative Bill Carter is Billy, Jim Keffer is Jimmy, and even Scott Hochberg, a Jewish wonk from Houston whose idea of a good time is a Saturday afternoon working on public-education funding formulas, is Scottie.

When it looked like welfare reform was dead, Naishtat was called over to meet with Bush and his chief legislative aide. "The governor wanted to know what was wrong with permanent disqualification for felony drug possession," Naishtat said. "I told him that in Texas, you can be convicted of a felony for possession of one gram of cocaine. That could mean the children of a mother who is caught riding in a car with a man who has a gram of cocaine will be permanently barred from benefits." Naishtat argued for a "three-year freeze-out," which would allow a woman convicted of possession to serve her prison time, then have some support for her children when she got out. Bush said he would think about it. Naishtat quickly got the word that the governor had to have permanent disqualification. "I think he was sincere and sympathetic to my argument," Naishtat said. "Maybe if he hadn't been running for president, he would have gone along with the three-year freeze-out rather than permanent disqualification."

Why was a nice guy with a drug history of his own such a hard-ass? Late in the session, Naishtat was in the House members' lounge when Bush's legislative director, Terral Smith, walked in and pleaded with Naishtat and another Austin state rep, Glen Maxey, to move the stalled welfare bill out of the Human Services Committee.

"Terral walked into the members' lounge," Maxey said. "He must have forgotten he was no longer a member of the House. And he said we had to get the bill to the Calendars Committee and that the governor needed the punitive measures so that Pat Buchanan wouldn't be able to beat him up in the Republican primaries."

During most of W. Bush's governorship, the welfare allowance in Texas was $188 a month for a woman with two children. Not $188 a week; $188 a month. On October 1, 1999, that sum soared to $201 a month, putting us ahead of

Alabama and Louisiana. The increase was no thanks to Bush, who wanted the money for his property-tax cut. The dirty secret of Texas government is that we keep our "low tax, low services" tradition going by cheating the poor. According to a September 1999 Census Bureau study, Texas has the highest rate of people with no health insurance in the country, 25 percent. In October 1999, Families USA found that the number of Texas children enrolled in Medicaid declined by 14 percent between 1996 and 1999, the largest decline in the twelve states studied. A typical case was reported by the *Austin American-Statesman*: "Having recently endured the application process for Texas Medicaid, Kim Piseno isn't surprised that 598,000 kids from low-income families who are eligible for the health insurance program aren't enrolled. Pregnant and with little income, Piseno knew she was eligible for prenatal care through the program. But first the eighteen-year-old had to find her birth certificate—no mean feat because she had run away when she was twelve. She also had to present proof of pregnancy and records showing income and total financial assets. After waiting months for a response from the Department of Human Services, she was told that her papers had been lost and that she'd have to apply again."

Welfare reform isn't the only issue that makes Bush sound like Tom DeLay on a bad day. Early in the 1999 session, Bush decided to drastically limit a children's health-insurance program by declaring that only children in families below 150 percent of the federal poverty level would qualify for low-cost health insurance through the Children's Health Insurance Program. CHIP, as the program is known, receives $2.84 in federal dollars for each state dollar spent. Other Republican governors, including Florida's Jeb Bush, were setting eligibility at 200 percent. Governor Christine Todd Whitman set 300 percent as New Jersey's eligibility level. Yet Texas, second to California in the number of uninsured children, was fighting to keep kids out of a health-insurance program that would cost the state approximately $189 million—in funds waiting to be drawn from the interest on the state's share of the tobacco lawsuit.

House Democrats wanted to set the eligibility at 200 percent of the federal poverty level. The percentages make a big difference. There are 1.4 million children in Texas who have no health insurance. With eligibility at 200 percent, 500,000 could be insured. At the 150 percent the governor wanted, only 300,000 could buy the subsidized insurance. "CHIP was a program that could have been implemented in 1997 with a signature from the governor," Maxey said. "Children could have already been enrolled. But the governor decided to appoint a committee to study the problem."

What the committee—or the Bush campaign advisers— found is that CHIP is a Medicaid magnet. Once it's advertised, children show up, only to be told their families earn too little to qualify for CHIP, but the children automatically qualify for Medicaid. "The real fear was the Medicaid spillover," Maxey said. When Bush realized the legislators weren't going to let him deny 200,000 kids health insurance, his office began to fight for separate applications for CHIP and Medicaid. In other words, if CHIP applicants qualified for Medicaid, they would have to make an appointment at a Medicaid office and fill out another application. And that application is difficult and complicated, requiring applicants to prove they have less than $2,000 in total assets. "All the studies show that 66 percent never return," Maxey said.

In straightforward, nonbureaucratic English, because he is running for president, George Bush attempted to (1) bar 200,000 children from a low-cost federal-state health-insurance program, and (2) discourage poor children from receiving free health care to which they are entitled under federal law. "They were terrified of the Medicaid spillover because they want to be able to say welfare rolls are dropping," Maxey said. "They know that a lot of the children who show up for CHIP insurance will end up qualifying for Medicaid. And that means enrollment will start to climb in the middle of the campaign."

After House Democrats prevailed with 200 percent eligibility and one application for both CHIP and Medicaid, Bush walked out to Representative Glen Maxey's desk on the House floor, placed both hands on his shoulders, and congratulated him for his hard work on children's health insurance. "You shoved it down our throat," the governor said as the press pack watched.

Glen Maxey is a master of "close-talking"—the *entre nous* conversational technique that implies absolute confidence and intimacy among legislators and lobbyists. He is also the only openly gay member of the Texas House and represents the district in which the governor resides. On this particular April afternoon, the governor outdid Maxey in close-talking, pulling his state rep to within whispering distance and saying, according to Maxey, "I value you as a person, and I value you as a human being, and I want you to know, Glen, that what I say publicly about gay people doesn't pertain to you."

Maxey was stunned. "Skippy, the little ACT UP devil that sits on my shoulder, was telling me, 'Kiss him,'" Maxey said. Instead, he told his constituent that when he says gays are not qualified to be adoptive parents, "you are talking about me, because I'm gay."

Maxey immediately told the House members standing around him what Bush had said. The governor's press office denies that Bush made the remarks, so we're left with a swearing match between a press functionary and a legislator. But Bush's policy on gays and lesbians is straightforward: He's against them.

He supported the gay-adoption-ban bill filed by Panhandle Republican Warren Chisum, a likeable, avuncular homophobe who's usually good for one or two anti-gay bills each session. In 1997 it was gay marriage. In 1999 it was a ban on gays and lesbians as adoptive or foster parents. The governor supported it, saying that children belonged in traditional two-parent families.

To the national press, gay and lesbian marriage and adoption bans in state legislatures are so common that they are considered background noise generated by the Christian right. But when James Byrd, Jr., was chained to a pickup truck and dragged to his death in the summer of 1998, the networks, the newsweeklies, and the nation's big dailies all came to Jasper, Texas (as they traveled to Wyoming, to cover the fence-post crucifixion of a young gay man named Matthew Shepard).

Less than a year after Byrd's brutal murder, the demand in the black, brown, and gay communities for a hate-crimes law was something Bush had to deal with. And he did; he opposed it, saying that all crimes of violence are hate crimes so no special categories of victims should be created.

After the Texas House overwhelmingly passed the James Byrd Jr. Hate Crimes Bill and the national press began to pay attention, Bush said he would consider the bill if the Senate passed it. Then he quietly worked to keep it bottled up in a Senate committee, where Florence Shapiro, a Dallas-area Republican whose home was once defaced by a swastika, did his bidding.

"The bill is stuck in the Senate Criminal Justice Committee because committee Republicans could not accept gays and lesbians as a special category," Rodney Ellis, the bill's Senate sponsor, told reporters covering the story. Ellis refused to consider a hate-crimes bill that would not protect gays and lesbians—who are 30 percent of the victims of hate crimes reported nationwide. So Ellis and the governor's office were at an impasse. Because the gay and lesbian category would offend Christian-right voters who make up one third of the Republican primary vote, Ellis' hate-crimes bill was dying in committee.

Ellis reminded reporters that several of the same senators who were blocking the bill had voted for the exact same bill two years earlier, when it couldn't get through the House— and when the governor was not running for president. Senate supporters of the bill organized a media campaign and brought in Renee Mullins, a daughter of James Byrd, Jr., and survivors of lesser-known hate crimes, to plead with committee Republicans. After two weeks of hearings, the bill's supporters won over the Republicans on the Criminal Justice Committee.

Since Bush had authorized almost one hundred executions by the time the legislative session wound down, it was hard to argue that Texas needed to create a new capital offense. In fact, the James Byrd Jr. Hate Crimes Bill was a bad law filled with dangerous provisions, including an expansion of the death penalty. But it was a bad bill that was desperately needed—if only to reassure minority communities that the government cares about what happens to them. (And, we might point out, this would not have been the first bad law ever passed by the Texas Legislature.)

Once the deal was done, the committee had to move to a larger hearing room to accommodate the media and the supporters of the bills who showed up to witness the final vote. It was quite a show, as the committee Republicans returned from their caucus meeting with a representative of the governor's office and voted to kill the bill.

Democrats then attempted to hold the Senate hostage, walking out and holding a pray-in under the capitol dome. Dozens of bills died during each of the ten hours they kept the Senate shut down on the final day committees could act on bills. But they were killing bills they had worked on themselves for four and a half months, so after ten hours of failed negotiations they came back in.

Two hundred bills died, the Legislature was shut down for a day, and the level of personal animosity in the genteel Texas Senate reached levels not seen for years. Moments after the bill was declared dead, one of the Senate's moderate Republicans handed out a press release stating he had been secretly negotiating at the behest of the governor. It was not George Bush's finest half hour. Not even the Republicans bought it. To the bill's sponsor it was a joke. "Governor Bush never put no paper in my hand," Rodney Ellis said.

Not only did the fight over hate crimes have Senate Democrats walking out to sing and pray in the capitol rotunda, it also produced one of the more bizarre episodes in a state where we have a high standard for the bizarre. Renee Mullins traveled from Hawaii, where her husband is stationed at a military base, to testify before the Legislature and meet with the governor. The Senate Criminal Justice Committee heard her testimony, but Bush refused to see her. So Mullins decided to call Republican senator Kay Bailey Hutchison to ask for help. "I knew Senator Hutchison was the only Republican who attended her father's funeral," Diane Hardy-García said. Hardy-García occupies one of the lonelier positions in the capitol. She is the lobbyist for the Lesbian & Gay Political Caucus, and as such, she spent the early months of the '99 session pushing the hate-crimes bill through Lege. After the bill passed the House, she struggled to move it through the Senate committee. She brought Mullins to Austin and also knew Mullins had talked to the senator several times by phone. "I didn't think she would get through in time," Hardy-García said, "until she told me she had Hutchison's home phone number." Mullins called the senator, and within hours Bush changed his mind.

It was probably a mistake. According to Hardy-García, who accompanied Mullins to the meeting, the governor seemed very uncomfortable. Mullins asked Bush why he opposed the bill, and he told her he hadn't read it. "She gave him a copy and he threw it on his desk," Hardy-García said. Then she asked, 'Will you help us?' He said, 'No.' "

"She was crying, and he didn't try to console her or even offer her a Kleenex," Hardy-García said. "He was cold, icy, to her."

Maybe the tone of the meeting was established when Representative Senfronia Thompson, an outspoken African-American from Houston known for her offbeat sense of humor, attempted a bit of levity. Thompson was the House sponsor of the hate-crimes bill, so she accompanied Mullins, Hardy-García, and several others to the meeting with the governor. Thompson looked up at a portrait on the wall of the governor's mansion. It was a mustachioed man in military dress. "Oh, my God. Is that Hitler?" she asked. Bush said it wasn't and must have regretted that he had agreed to meet with Mullins.

Since the bidness of bidness is bidness,* and bidness will always be taken care of in the Texas Legislature, you have to measure a governor by asking how much political capital he is willing to exhaust on behalf of those outside the bidness community. What's the governor willing to do on behalf of what some of us still rather naïvely refer to as the public interest?

You don't need a Ph.D. from the LBJ School for this one either: Dubya takes care of bidness. While he was fighting to deny children health care at the beginning of the 1999 session, he was personally flogging the only bill he designated "emergency legislation": his $45 million tax break for owners of marginally productive oil and gas wells. "There's a lot of people hurting," said Bush, the bleeding heart. Bush sold this tax break as one that would benefit only the owners of itty-bitty oil wells. Turned out that most of the marginal wells were owned by Exxon.

When big-bidness interests clash at the capitol, an African proverb is sometimes cited: "When elephants fight, the grass suffers." In 1999 the session's "big elephant bill" was on

*It has occurred to us that spelling business "bidness" can be construed as nauseatingly cute. Years ago, an out-of-state bidness writer who had been to interview Trammell Crow, the Dallas real estate magnate, reported in astonishment, "Goddamn, I thought you were making that up—he really does say 'bidness'!" So does Ross Perot, as well as practically every other Texas magnate we've ever met. The point is not to mock the regional pronunciation, but to lend some emphasis to the peculiar political veneration accorded "bidness" in this state. If you were to substitute "Jesus" for "bidness," the effect in the Lege would not be much different.

deregulation of electric utilities. The bill stuck 70 percent of some $7 billion in "stranded costs"—debts the utilities ran up by building expensive nuclear plants—onto the bills of residential consumers. When Kevin Bailey, a puckish rep from Houston, passed a committee amendment forcing industrial and commercial consumers to pay 50 percent of the stranded costs, there was full-scale panic from Bush's staff. His legislative director, Terral Smith, raced into the hearing room and began working Republicans until he found someone to call for reconsideration of the pro-consumer amendment. It got so bad that when East Texas Republican Tommy Merritt—thinking he was voting on the amendment itself—voted "no" on reconsideration, Smith stepped onto the dais and made him change his vote.

Republicans on the committee were so offended by the crude lobbying that four of them stuck with the pro-consumer amendment, which survived. At a press conference on the following day, the governor said he opposed the amendment because "it threatens to derail the deregulation bill." When he was pressed to explain what was wrong with the content of the amendment, he said, "It's bad for business and will drive capital out of state." The deregulation bill passed, with a weakened version of Bailey's amendment, and Texas Utilities has yet to move its power plants to Minnesota.

A week later, as the 1999 legislative session ended, the entire omnibus welfare-reform bill died after the governor again tried to restore all the punitive measures he needed to keep Pat Buchanan off his back. There was no special session called to save welfare reform. The presidential campaign was beginning, and Bush had indicated he would call a "special" only if he didn't get his $262 million tax break for bidness—or if the education bill with his $1 billion in property-tax relief didn't make it out of an eleventh-hour conference committee.

The governor got both—but only after Democrats on the conference committee beat back an effort by Senate Republicans on behalf of the Education Governor to pull $250 million out of kindergarten funding to cover the tax breaks for business.

Another standard-issue example of how Bush takes care of bidness is the SCI matter, now under litigation. This one has some "heart-rendering" aspects, as they say in the Lege.

SCI stands for Service Corporation International, out of Houston, and they are the Exxon of the funeral home industry. While you have been paying no attention, these folks have been buying up your locally owned funeral parlors. Basically, this worldwide outfit is massive. The late Jessica Mitford, peerless student of the funeral industry, devoted an entire chapter to SCI in her updated version of *The American Way of Death*. SCI prefers to leave the names of local morticians on the parlors it acquires, but odds are you'll never get out of this world alive without paying SCI.

Its CEO is Robert Waltrip, a longtime friend of the Bush family's. He is a trustee of Bush the Elder's presidential library at Texas A&M and his company contributed $100,000 toward its construction. In 1998 Waltrip arranged for former president Bush to speak at a funeral home convention and SCI paid his $70,000 honorarium. He also gave $10,000 to W. Bush's first gubernatorial race, and SCI's political action committee gave $35,000 to his second. In Texas the funeral industry is regulated by a tiny agency, the

Funeral Service Commission, which had been a captive agency for years but was under pressure to get tough because of increasing complaints. The commission hired a new director, Eliza May, who had been active in Democratic Party politics. The commission had received complaints that two funeral homes were using unlicensed embalmers. Gayle Johnson, the mother of a popular television newsman in Wichita Falls, said SCI had failed to properly embalm her son's body. When she went to lay flowers at his mausoleum, she claimed, she found it infested with gnats and a smelly maroon liquid was leaking out of the crypt (a charge SCI denies).

May requested documents concerning the alleged violations from SCI; their lawyer said the company hadn't been told enough about the allegations and suggested she go to the funeral home premises. Four days later inspectors arrived at homes in Dallas and Fort Worth and asked for certain documents. When Waltrip heard about the raids, he went ballistic and mounted a blistering counterattack. He went to Austin to personally deliver a letter of protest to the commission and then proceeded to the governor's office to again complain of "storm trooper tactics" and ask that the commission staff be investigated. Bush stopped by while Waltrip was meeting with chief of staff Joe Allbaugh and said, "Hey, Bobby, are those people still messing with you?" according to an SCI lobbyist present at the time. He then asked the lobbyist, "Hey Johnnie B., are you taking care of him?"

Bush described the encounter as nonsubstantive. He says he was on his way to a press conference and very briefly stopped by the meeting. "It's a twenty-second conversation," Bush told the press. "I had no substantive conversation with the guy. I don't remember what I said, for starters. I poked my head in the office for no more than twenty seconds. And that's it. That's all that was discussed."

Within an hour of Waltrip's visit, May says she received a message to call Allbaugh. Over the next several weeks, May alleges in court documents, she received phone calls from three of Bush's senior aides asking her if she could wrap up the SCI investigation, and she was called to a meeting with Allbaugh and Senator John Whitmire, who represents Waltrip's home district and had received a total of $5,000 in campaign contributions from SCI. They demanded that she immediately turn over a list of the documents she needed to close the investigation. In August 1998, the Funeral Commission recommended fines of $450,000, the largest penalty ever assessed by the commission. SCI refused to pay, contending that the commission had misinterpreted state embalming laws. Shortly thereafter, the company got a ruling from Bush's close ally, Attorney General John Cornyn, which may allow SCI to avoid paying the penalty. Eliza May was fired in February and is suing the state, SCI, and Waltrip. SCI and Waltrip deny interfering with the commission's investigation or using political connections to have May fired. And Bush said he "never asked anyone to take a role or become involved in any way in this investigation or any dispute arising from it."

Reporters love a courthouse fight, in part because there is nothing like a lawsuit to put the truth on the public record. It is only because Eliza May's lawyers took sworn depositions from the SCI boys that the public got a glimpse of how business is taken care of when no one is around to watchdog the governor's staff. Even if Dubya's brief remarks were of "little substance," as he claims, they were a lot friendlier to the regulated industry than the regulator, who seemed to be doing her job.

Bush christened his campaign plane *Great Expectations,* but *TCB* for "Taking Care of Business"—as Elvis named his plane—might be more appropriate. Whether it's done quietly by the governor in his executive office, or openly by the governor's legislative director leaning on a junior member of the House, it is this service to the interests of big bidness that has been the hallmark of this governor.

The Bush team attends to the "entertainment issues," such as God, guns, and gays. But his political capital is invested in the issues that are dearest to the business community: tort reform, lax regulation of industrial polluters, tax cuts for the oil and gas industry, electricity rates that place the interests of industry far above the interests of consumers, and privatizing welfare for huge profit. Texas is a state with a history of chief executives who served the business community well. Few have done it quite so willingly as George W. Bush.

Is the Air Cleaner?
Bush and the Environment

*But Bush's environmental track record—
you know he's running on empty.*
—Neil Carman, Lone Star Sierra Club, May 1999

*You've got to ask the question, is the air cleaner since
I became governor? And the answer is yes.*
—George W. Bush, May 1999

That's not a stretcher—that's a whopper. If you want to get strong about it, it's a perverse distortion of reality, since Bush is, to put it mildly, part of the problem.

By no known standard has the air of Texas improved under Governor Bush, nor has anything else involving the environment. He personally intervened to protect major air polluters in the state, and his appointees in this area are staggeringly dreadful.

According to the tri-national North American Commission on Environmental Cooperation, set up by NAFTA, Texas pollutes more than any other state or Canadian province. That record includes air pollution and water pollution. We're number one.

And according to records kept by the Environmental Defense Fund, Texas is also number one in:

☆ overall toxic releases
☆ recognized carcinogens in the air
☆ suspected carcinogens in the air
☆ developmental toxins in the air (affecting brain and nervous-system development in children)
☆ cancer risk.

And number one in ten other categories of dangerous air pollutants in the environment too.

The problem was not created by Bush, and we have had governors who cared even less about it. In 1980 our then-governor Bill Clements' oil company owned the offshore rig that blew out in Mexico's Bay of Campeche, causing an immense oil slick to wash up on Texas beaches. As the slick approached land, Clements was asked what he thought we should do about it. "Pray for a hurricane," he snarled. (He did actually snarl—Clements snarled rather frequently.) Still, Bush's record is dismal, even by our standards.

The Texas Gulf Coast, from the Louisiana border south to Corpus Christi, is home to the largest concentration of refineries and chemical plants in the United States. The ungodly stench that afflicts coastal cities from Port Arthur to Port Aransas is described by residents as "the smell of money." It's sort of a combination of something chemical and something rotten. Again, the industries, the pollution they produce, and the smell existed long before Bush became governor, but it is fair to ask why he hasn't used his six years in office to do anything except let the problem get worse—and has even stymied efforts to improve it. Big George Bush asked a similar question in 1988, when he used Boston Harbor as a backdrop for a television ad that claimed Michael Dukakis was responsible for "500 million gallons of barely treated sewage and 70 tons of sludge" flowing into the harbor daily. Thanks to Bush the Younger, plants producing 904,000 tons of air pollution annually could continue to operate as they have for almost thirty years—in ways that would have them shut down or fined in almost any other state in the nation.

Since 1988 Boston Harbor has gotten a lot cleaner, as has the air in Los Angeles and the water in the Hudson River— all environmental success stories under Republican governors. It is not beyond expectation, it is not un-Republican, it is not even unusual for environmental progress to be made. In this state, Houston, Dallas, Fort Worth, El Paso, and Beaumont–Port Arthur have all been put on the EPA list of "nonattainment zones." (Now, there's a catchy bureaucratic phrase for you; it means the air is filthy and air alerts have to be issued on a regular basis in the summertime.) In addition, Austin, Tyler, San Antonio, and Longview are now eligible to be on the list, having attained the appropriate levels of pollution, but they have not yet worked their way through the bureaucracy. Dallas–Fort Worth is now listed as a serious nonattainment zone and is expected to move up to severe. As L.A.'s air gets better, Houston's gets worse, and on at least one indicator, Houston has already beat L.A. for "most polluted": In 1998 and 1999 Houston had the single highest recorded ozone levels of any city in the country. A study done by the city of Houston itself shows air pollution causes at least 430 deaths per year, another kind of death penalty.

Between 1993 and 1998, fifty-six of the ninety-six nonattainment areas around the country got off that list; none were in Texas. It's harder to tell about the pollution of Texas rivers, because after Bush got elected governor, the state virtually stopped monitoring water quality. The pesticide-monitoring program has also been largely abandoned; according to the EPA, 59 million pounds of pesticides were used in Texas in 1998.

Bush began briskly in 1995 by calling for the resignation of all three of Ann Richards' appointees to the Texas Natural Resources Conservation Commission, the closest thing Texas has to an EPA. The commission is known in state government as Trainwreck, since that's the closest we can come to pronouncing the acronym TNRCC. It was established in the early nineties to monitor air quality and to grant state permits for new refineries, chemical and industrial plants, and landfills. Trainwreck was never a center of environmental activism, to put it mildly. But by the end of Bush's first term, it had clearly become what government professors call "a captive regulatory agency"—controlled by the industries it was established to regulate.

Richards' appointees to Trainwreck were a man (just for the record, African-American) with more than a decade's experience as an administrator in state environmental agencies; a woman county commissioner from Austin, a town notoriously full of tree huggers and whale savers; and a woman county judge from West Texas, where they equally notoriously do not hug trees—they don't even have trees. Bush replaced this trio with three white guys so sympathetic to big polluters it left Texas environmentalists whomper-jawed. John Baker is from the Texas Farm Bureau, the agricultural interest group that sells discount insurance and tires to farmers and ranchers. Although the bureau purports to speak for Texas farmers, it is actually a large insurance company whose portfolio is loaded with agricultural chemical stocks. The bureau has opposed all efforts to regulate pesticides in Texas. The next new commissioner was Ralph Marquez, who spent thirty years working for the Monsanto chemical company and then became a lobbyist for the Texas Chemical Council. The man from Monsanto went to Washington, D.C., using his position as one of Texas' top environmental officials, to testify that ozone is "benign"; he opposed efforts to strengthen federal air-quality standards. And finally, the man who may well replace Carole Browner at EPA should Bush become president, our Barry McBee.

McBee is a boyish lawyer in his mid-forties who worked in Bush the Elder's White House. He was called back to Texas by Rick Perry in 1994. Perry, he of the good hair, now lieutenant governor, had then just been elected state ag comissioner. If Karl Rove is Bush's brain, McBee is certainly Rick Perry's gray matter. He's a smart technocrat who has spent most of his life in government and is also an evangelical Christian who would occasionally fall to his knees and pray before casting a vote to open a corporate hog farm in the Panhandle. At one Trainwreck meeting in 1997, McBee launched into a homily on Christian love and mercy just before casting a landfill vote; a major industry lobbyist said later, "It absolutely scared the shit out of everybody in the business community."

"I do hope that people would say and know that I am a Christian," McBee told a reporter in 1997. He is the perfect W. Bushie, a combination of Christian and corporate. In the Texas Senate, to which McBee transferred after his old boss Perry was elected lite guv, McBee is known as "the skinny Hitler." They're colorful in the Texas Senate.

Bush's appointees to Trainwreck spent tens of thousands of dollars lobbying against and rallying industry opposition to the new federal air-quality health standards enacted in

1997. Before November of '97 they made many trips around the state for meetings with people from industry, urging them to write their congressmen. They held "rallies" where six to eight people showed up, all happy to denounce the feds.

Rebecca Flores-Harrington, now with the AFL-CIO, spent many years organizing for Cesar Chavez's United Farm Workers. In 1986, when Jim Hightower, a populist Democrat, was elected state ag commissioner, Flores worked with him to develop a policy requiring farmers to warn workers when fields sprayed with pesticides were so "hot" they could cause illness or even death. One worker had already died of pesticide exposure, offed like a bug sprayed with Raid. "The policy was really nothing radical," said Flores. "We just wanted signs posted that would warn workers that a field has been sprayed, and that for two or three days the fresh, active chemicals in the field could kill them."

When McBee went to work as deputy director of the Texas Department of Agriculture, one of his first acts was to dismantle the right-to-know regulations that protected farmworkers. "It took us years to get the system to work for us," said Flores. "He took it apart in one day."

According to a 1999 study, "Pesticides and Texas Water Quality" by the Texas Center for Policy Studies, the number of pesticide stations sampled went from twenty-seven in 1985 (under Hightower) to one in 1997. The report details many other inadequacies in the monitoring program.

When Bush moved McBee to Trainwreck, the agency reduced public participation in its hearings. That policy was challenged by a grain farmer from the Panhandle, who vehemently opposed the granting of a permit for a corporate hog farm across the road from his house. He sued and won his right—and the right of all citizens—to participate in permit hearings. However, Trainwreck has recently published rules trying to get around the court order and close the hearings again. Meanwhile, Texas is going in the opposite direction from other states like Iowa, Oklahoma, and North Carolina on large, confined animal-feed operations, particularly hog farms. These outfits produce enormous amounts of fecal waste that threatens water supplies and water quality. While other states are tightening regulation of the waste, Texas has been moving to cut the operations free of regulation. The agency also began providing advance notice of "surprise inspections" of large industrial facilities, thus lending a surprising new meaning to *surprise*. Trainwreck also opposed the EPA's attempts to strengthen national air-quality standards and all but simply stopped monitoring water quality in the state's rivers and streams.

As bad as Trainwreck was under Bush, the commissioners finally decided something had to be done about the state's grandfathered refineries, utilities, and chemical and industrial plants. These plants are exempt from state pollution controls because they were in operation before the Texas Clean Air Act went into effect in 1971. Former state representative Sissy Farenthold says the grandfather exemption was meant to be for "a few years, maybe four," giving the plants enough time to come up to the new state standards. Twenty-eight years later, the same 850 plants are producing 36 percent—more than one third—of the state's total air pollution. The Environmental Defense Fund, the Sierra Club, and the Public Citizen group have worked for years to increase public awareness of the issue, and pressure on Trainwreck gradually increased. Not just greens were involved;

because every one of the state's major metropolitan areas is or soon will be declared in "nonattainment," the EPA's immortal euphemism, that means the loss of highway funds. That's a BFD, as they say in East Texas (big f—ing deal), in a state where highway spending has precedence over all other state functions, including the public schools and public health. The EPA designation also leads to some restrictions on business.

Just as Trainwreck was about to crack down on the grandfathered plants, Bush stepped in. The Sierra Club and an environmental coalition called SEED got the following information through an open-records request. In 1997 Bush's environmental director warned the governor that industry was concerned that his three appointees to Trainwreck, those environmental firebrands, were "moving too quickly" and "may rashly seek legislation this session." Within a few months the governor quietly asked two oil-company presidents to outline a voluntary program for the grandfathered polluters, which is something like asking criminals to set the length of their own sentences. In June 1997 the same two oil execs summoned two dozen industry representatives to a meeting at Exxon's corporate headquarters in Houston and handed them an outline of the voluntary emissions-reduction plan Bush had requested. A memo written by a DuPont executive who attended the meeting indicates some astonishment: "The approach of the presenters was pretty much like, 'This is the way it's going to be. Do you want to get on board or not?' Clearly the insiders from oil & gas believe that the Governor's Office will 'persuade' the TNRCC to accept what program is developed between the industry group and the Governor's Office."

And they did. The governor of the state with the highest

volume of air pollution in the nation accommodated the state's biggest polluters. After almost three decades of unrestrained pollution, he let it continue under the guise of "voluntary compliance." Of the 850 grandfathered polluters, 28 have come up with a plan to reduce pollution, but only 3 have actually done so. Hell of a program.

Two years after his 1997 gift to oil, gas, and electric utilities, Bush moved to have his voluntary-emissions program written into law. In what could be his last legislative effort in Texas, his staff beat back a revolt by House Democratic liberals against setting this nonsense into law. The D's put up a bill requiring the plants to use what environmental engineers call the Best Available Control Technology. The governor's office had its own bill, written by R. Kinnan Goleman, a lobbyist for energy and utility companies who is also general counsel for the Texas Chemical Council. Goleman's bill permitted the use of ten-year-old pollution-control technology and *voluntary* compliance with the law. Every newspaper in the state ran angry editorials opposing this joke of a bill. Despite the eleventh-hour stand by the Democrats, the deal went down.

Two campaign-finance watchdog groups, Public Research Works and the Center for Responsive Politics, discovered this happy concordance: The companies participating in the industry working group that helped design Bush's voluntary program gave a total of $260,648 to his 1998 gubernatorial campaign—and $243,900 to his presidential campaign within a month of the opening of his exploratory committee. The largest donor to Bush's last race for governor was a South Texas oil-and-gas operator who gave $101,000. Among those who contributed over $75,000 that year were four energy company CEOs, for a total of $325,000.

After Bush's bill—written by the lobbyist who represents Exxon, Koch Industries, ASARCO, etc.—had been passed by the House, its sponsor, Representative Ray Allen of Grand Prairie, explained to a colleague why he had carried it: "to protect Texas Utilities [a Dallas company]—and to make George Bush green for the presidential campaign." Although some House Republicans actually claimed the bill was pro-environment, the only green involved was money.

The height of Bush's environmental greenery came late in the '99 legislative session. He said during a press conference, "Yes, I think global warming is a problem." As it happens, Texas leads the nation in the emission of carbon monoxide, the principal greenhouse gas. But the American Petroleum Institute immediately declared itself "surprised" by this ferociously green stand. A spokesman for an industry-funded "grassroots" group complained of "a shock wave through the community." Sierra Club spokesman Neil Carman was driven to mix his metaphors: "But Bush's environmental track record—you know he's running on empty," he told the *Fort Worth Star-Telegram*. Dan Quayle jumped fearlessly into the fray, claiming Dubya was "surrendering." So Bush retreated, saying a few days later that while his environmental advisers agree there is "some warming, they disagree about its cause and impact."

Just one more indicator on air quality—the number of days when Texas cities violated the one-hour ozone count. For the four years Richards was governor, the numbers are 58, 43, 38, and 48. The numbers for Bush's first term are 88, 38, 69, and 56. Of the twenty-one air-quality indices looked at by the Environmental Defense Fund, all have gotten worse under Bush.

For twenty years the state of Texas has been trying to get

the EPA to let it take over the Federal Water Pollution Permit Program, known by another nonacronym, Nipdes, for National Pollution Discharge Elimination System. Without federal approval of the state's water-pollution control program, all the industries and cities in Texas have to get two water-pollution permits—one from Trainwreck and one from EPA. This is not only annoying but costly, running into thousands of dollars per permit. Industry could save money and local governments could cut costs as well if Texas just had a water-pollution program that measured up to federal standards. Every year Texas would apply to take over the program, and every year the EPA would reject its application, pointing out all the inadequacies in the Texas program. Every year the state would fix a couple of things out of the hundreds that were wrong and then reapply hopefully. Back it would come, again listing all the problems yet to be fixed. In 1997 the EPA listed seventy pages' worth of problems with the Texas application, including several laws passed in the 1995 session that created new problems in water-pollution control. Texas was one of seven states that failed to get EPA approval. But all the while congressional pressure on the agency was building; Texas congressmen wrote angry letters again and again. The Legislature finally moved to fix some of the problems listed by the EPA, and the application was approved in 1998, to the horror of Texas environmentalists, who promptly filed a lawsuit.

The suit, filed by the Sierra Club and Clean Water Action, notes, among other pesky considerations, that (1) Texas doesn't provide adequate resources in either money or people to do the job, spending even less than Louisiana; (2) our Texas "voluntary" compliance program does not meet EPA's enforcement criteria; and (3) there's not enough public participation allowed in the permit process to ensure proper consideration of applications.

Texas has water-quality data for only a small percentage of its streams and rivers. The state has over 190,000 miles of streams and rivers, but only 40,000 are perennial, meaning they flow year-round. The state has designated specific uses—for example, water supply, contact recreation, high-quality aquatic life, etc.—for only 14,385 stream miles, about 7.5 percent of the total. Those 14,385 miles are called "classified segments"—yet another bureaucratic gift to the language—and the only water-quality monitoring we have is on these classified segments. In 1995 the number of monitoring stations was decreased by 24 percent. About 86 percent of the 446 existing water-quality monitoring stations are checked four times a year, the rest less frequently. Of the classified stream miles, 72.2 percent met the qualifications for their designated use in 1992; 66 percent in 1994; and 67.9 percent in 1996. Perhaps the most ominous drop in water quality is in classified reservoirs. In 1992, 90 percent of the classified reservoirs fully supported their designated use; in 1994, 98 percent; and in 1996, 78 percent. According to Trainwreck, this "substantial decline in reservoir water quality statewide" was due to low dissolved-oxygen levels (affecting aquatic life), elevated fecal coliform (basically, that's shit, and it affects contact recreation use), and elevated levels of metals and organic pollutants. In addition, the Texas Department of Health issued fish-consumption bans for several reservoirs because of mercury contamination.

According to a coalition of Texas enviros reporting on the state's perennial Nipdes application in 1996, Texas ranks at the top of every criterion of need for a strong water-pollution program.

☆ It ranks number one in major discharge facilities (those are your big-time polluters), with 575 major facilities, compared with the next-largest states of Pennsylvania with 390 and New York with 350 major facilities.

☆ Texas ranks second in total number of minor Nipdes facilities, about 5,700. Louisiana has the largest number of such facilities in the country, about 6,000.

☆ Texas is the second-most populous state, but it has very limited water resources. Many of the state rivers, lakes, and bays are severely polluted. Over 3,000 miles, or one third, of Texas rivers and 44 percent of Texas bays are so polluted that they do not meet the standards set for recreational and other uses. Thirteen Texas lakes were covered by advisories or bans on fish consumption in 1996.

Kristen Warren, executive director of the Texas League of Conservation Voters, said sadly, "Environmentalists around the country really want to believe Bush is good on the environment. When they ask me about him, it makes me feel bad that I have to tell them the truth."

Bush has signed numerous bills that weaken environmental protection. Most of the anti-environmental agenda of the Republican Revolution of 1994, which failed to pass in Washington, has passed and is law in Texas, including bills concerning takings, audit/privilege immunity, cost-benefit analysis, regulatory flexibility, and reduction of the public's right to participate. The takings bill in particular, a pet project of the wacko right favored by militias everywhere, threatens to become a monumental problem for the state.

But perhaps the apogee of environmental folly during the Bush years was the Tejas Testing fiasco. By 1995, Houston, Dallas, El Paso, and other cities were in violation of

EPA air-pollution standards and the state was fixing to start the cleanup process by testing automobiles and making everybody ratchet down the pollution their cars cause. Of course, the only reason the state was doing this was so we could get back our highway money from the feds. But a right-wing radio host in Houston went on a jihad about how this was unconscionable government interference in our lives, and we have a right to breathe dirty air, and so on.* State senator John Whitmire, a peerless political opportunist, seized on this little quasi-populist flapette and made himself the champion of all those who felt heavy burdened by having to get their mufflers fixed. By then the state had not only signed a contract with Tejas Testing Technology, but the company also had sixty-five testing centers set up with all the equipment required to test emissions—just as the state contract required. Cooler heads warned Whitmire and those who joined him in this rebellion against Big Brother that the state would get sued if the contract was broken. But Bush backed Whitmire, and both pooh-poohed the idea we'd have to pay for it. Bush's support was critical. Tejas Testing went into bankruptcy as soon as the contract was broken and sued for $200 million, finally settling at $140 million. Now here's the beauty part. How to pay off this company? By using the funds appropriated to keep the air clean, of course. They took $41 million out of the Clean Air account, $63.6 million out of the Petroleum Storage Tank Remediation Fund, $20 million out of Hazardous

---

*This is not an original argument in the Lege. Representative Billy Williamson of Tyler, home to an infamous killer asbestos plant, once said on the floor, "I think we are all willing to have a little bit of crud in our lungs and a full stomach rather than a whole bunch of clean air and nothing to eat. And I don't want a bunch of environmentalists and Communists telling me what's good for me and my family." Billy has since died of lung cancer.

Solid Waste Remediation, and $10 mill out of general revenue. The remainder was put off to the next biennium, when they raided Clean Air funds again. Believe it or not, even the Chemical Council, which pays into the Superfund for hazardous-waste site cleanup, was pissed off about it. The state was out more than $140 million, and not a single nickel of it went to make the air cleaner. It was reckless and stupid. You talk about not stopping to think through the consequences of policy. Not only is our air that much dirtier, but now what the state needs is an emissions-testing program. And the air in Houston is so filthy people are rising up to demand one.

The Bright Spot:
Bush and Education

*I urge you to fund teacher training so our teachers learn to
teach reading with the most up-to-date science: phonics.*
—George W. Bush in his 1999 State of the State address

Education is one area where George W. Bush deserves real
credit, but oddly enough, not for what he is claiming credit
for. It's particularly annoying that he has made major campaign points out of phony claims, but he has been attentive,
consistent, and a hard worker to make public schools a
higher priority for the state. He has continued the reforms
that had already begun to make a real difference for the
public schools. During legislative battles, he responded to
every call and personally visited with state lawmakers in an
effort to shape better education policy for the state. The fact
that he lost on the one big thing he tried is a shame but no
discredit to him. Republicans and Democrats alike praise
him for his diligence and accessibility on all education issues. Again, because of the weakness of his office, it is impossible to give him the lion's share of the credit for any

single initiative—too much of the heavy lifting has been done by others. Likewise, in the one sad failure to improve schools during his tenure, he should not be blamed—especially since his efforts during that episode went beyond the call of duty. On this issue he has been bipartisan in the best tradition of the Texas Legislature, actually working more effectively with Democrats than with many members of his own party.

In addition to his impressive performance in the context of the Legislature on education issues, he has used the bully pulpit, one of the few real powers of his office. According to Bush's press office, in 1998 alone he made forty-seven speeches on education, almost one a week. Schools are easily his favorite campaign photo op, but he also visits them to dramatize education issues even when he's not running. He enjoys fielding the wacky questions kids ask. Another player who deserves credit here is Bush's wife, Laura. She is a former librarian who has chosen reading as her particular concern, the one she promotes in her role as first lady of the state. She is a shy person for whom speaking in public was, initially, almost visibly painful; but she has become an effective if not a rousing speaker on the subject of teaching children to read. Her sincerity and concern often make a deeper impression than more polished oratory.

But the record does need to be set straight concerning two of Bush's most dubious claims. The first is that he, himself, George W. Bush, "ended social promotion in Texas." It's a silly damn thing to say. Social promotion is the practice of promoting a student to the next grade along with his age group, even when the student's academic skills are clearly insufficient. Social promotion has been illegal in Texas since 1984. There is literally a law requiring school districts to ensure that students are performing at grade level before they can be promoted. In 1998 this was quietly pointed out to Bush, since his platform consisted largely of the pledge that he would see to it that "every child in Texas is able to read by the end of the third grade." Since they're already required to be at grade level before they can go on, this was an equally fatuous claim. But the campaign message resonated well with voters, so he went right on using it.

The only change concerning social promotion under the Bush administration flies directly in the face of Bush's often-stated philosophy that we should "trust local people to make right choices about their schools and cities." And it is a change deplored by educators around the state. Pre–George W., the law left up to local school districts how they would determine whether a student had adequate skills to be promoted to the next grade. We are talking here about K through 8, as they say in school jargon, since high school promotion is based on earned course credits. In Houston, for example, the policy was that a child could not be promoted unless he met two of the following criteria: (1) passing class grades; (2) passing the Texas Assessment of Academic Skills (TAAS) test; and (3) passing a nationally recognized academic-skills test. We could find no educators who support using one single criterion to determine a young child's academic fate.

But Bush began the 1999 session with a simple-minded solution to a nonexistent problem: require every child to pass the TAAS test before being promoted to the next grade. The trouble with that simple solution is that not all children do well at test-taking. It's an extreme notion to base a third-grader's total chance of promotion to the fourth grade on how she performs on one test, taken on a single day, when she might be ill or emotionally upset. In addition to taking away flexibility and choice from "local people," the downside of ending social promotion is that it increases the dropout rate, as countless studies have shown. So many educators showed up to protest Bush's simplistic approach that the Lege finally compromised, requiring children to pass either TAAS or some other state-approved test.

What we have done is make a single annual test the most important event in every young Texan's life. We envision a happy future for shrinks working on "test anxiety syndrome." The message to teacher is "Teach the test," and the message to kids is "Learn how to pass the test." This is not education.

The emphasis on this single test is beginning to make some legislators nervous, and several are calling for a reevaluation of TAAS. The TAAS test was originally designed as a way to measure how the state's 7,000 schools and 1,120 school districts compare with one another in educating children. It was not intended to be the final judge for children. It is, however, the foundation of the "accountability system" in Texas schools and has indeed been helpful for that purpose. TAAS was instituted by Skip Meno, Ann Richards' education commissioner, in 1991. The program was still considered an experiment when Bush came in, and many feared he would scrap it. He has instead supported and strengthened it. The good news is, and again Bush deserves credit for this, the Lege appropriated money for summer-reading programs for "at-risk" kids, which means "poor" in education jargon.

Bush's first foray into education policy was not a happy one. He ran in 1994 calling for less government regulation of schools and more local innovation; he was a great promoter of "charter schools." So during the 1995 session, the Lege set up a pilot program to fund twenty charter schools that would be free of most state regulation, including teacher certification. The idea was to give parents and local educators the freedom to fit the school to the children in the community. The charter schools receive state funds, as do regular public schools, based on average daily attendance—so much per head. The purpose of making it a pilot program was so the first twenty schools could be evaluated before more were considered.

But Bush liked his pet program so much, he pushed for expansion in 1997, before any evaluation could begin. The first seventeen charter schools opened their doors in the fall of 1996, so not even a full school year had passed before he asked for more. But Bush got what he wanted from the Lege, and his staff began pushing the Texas Education Agency to approve additional charters as rapidly as possible. At that time, the charter division of the TEA had two employees. The final decision on approval of the schools lay with the State Board of Education, with its fifteen elected members.* So despite painfully inadequate staff and a board with no guidelines or criteria, the number of charter schools exploded from 17 to 168 in just six months.

*The Board of Education is a painful subject in Texas. Texas voters like being able to choose all state officials rather than having them appointed by somebody else they voted for. But the voters' attention does tend to wander when they get far down-ballot, so they have an incurable tendency to elect people with names like Roy Rogers or Cyclone Davis. For some years now the board has been the target of "stealth candidates" from the Christian right. Seven of the fifteen members are now Christian right, and they are sometimes joined by one or another of the "secular members" to do odd things. Not just predictable things, like pushing phonics and school prayer; the Christian-right board members forced the state to dump its stock in the Walt Disney Company, which had been paying extremely handsome returns into the state school fund, on grounds they didn't like the company's allowing a gay pride day at Disneyland. (Or maybe it was the

One applicant for a charter was Ida Pinkard of Waco, a former postal employee with no experience in education other than being a mother and grandmother. Her résumé said she had taken some courses at a community college but had not graduated. Nevertheless, she was given a charter for the Emma L. Harrison School in Waco, which opened in 1998 to serve kids K through 9 with its seventeen teachers. Enrollment was initially at least two hundred children, most of them African-American. Since the school's records are a shambles, it is impossible to estimate average daily attendance, but the school got $750,000 in state funds based on Pinkard's estimate of the number of students.

The first clue that something was amiss came when the school failed to get its request for textbooks in to the state until October. By mid-December, the teachers' paychecks had started to bounce, as had those given to local vendors by the school. Word of these problems began to spread, and in January all but one of the school's board members resigned. The *Waco Tribune-Herald* began writing about the problems in February, whereupon Ida Pinkard banned the media from her campus. At which point even officials in Austin realized there was an ox in the ditch. The TEA dispatched a special master (who is appointed by the court and

---

Satanic message in the clouds shown in *The Lion King;* sometimes it's hard to tell.) The latest fight is an inexplicable effort to dump one money-management firm for the school fund in favor of another. For years the Board of Ed chose the school textbooks in a procedure dominated by . . . how to put this? . . . batshit right-wingers, who saw secular humanism in every picture of a woman not wearing an apron. (We do not exaggerate.) Because the state of Texas is such an enormous market, all the national textbook publishers have to meet Texas standards, which is why a generation of American students never heard of Eleanor Roosevelt or the United Nations, mention of which our Board of Ed considered prima facie evidence of Communist intent. The Lege eventually solved most of the problem by simply taking away much of the board's authority. Vestigial problems keep cropping up, however.

has the authority to take over a public entity), an experienced superintendent, and financial auditors to get a handle on the situation. The special master recommended that the school be closed as soon as possible. The records were a mess and contracts nonexistent, and school funds had been mingled with those of a community center. The final audit showed the Emma L. Harrison charter school almost $400,000 in debt, including about $83,000 owed to the IRS, and Social Security and Medicare on employees' wages.

The kids? Only 11 out of 103 who took the TAAS test passed it.

In another case, a charter school took the money, trained teachers, gussied up an old building, and was then broke. No students were ever admitted. Four other charter schools "forgot" to give the TAAS test. All of this could have been avoided if Bush had heeded the advice he was emphatically given—to move slowly so that adjustments in the program could be made as needed. Some charter schools may work out well in the long run. But not in time to save the children in Waco from a lost year. As nearly as the rest of the charter schools can be judged after so short a time, they follow the same pattern as regular public schools: Those in high socioeconomic areas have kids doing very well, those in low socioeconomic areas have kids doing less well.

Without extrapolating too much from one scarred program, this is an example of Bush's cavalier attitude about governance—policy simply does not interest him. He told Tucker Carlson, "Sitting down and reading a 500-page book on public policy or philosophy or something" is what he likes least. Again, the puzzle of Bush is why someone with so little interest in or attention for policy, for making government work, would want the job of president, or even governor.

Yet his political skills can make him a valuable player if he's interested, as he is in education. The Noble Effort of '97 is an example, but it requires a brief history of modern education reform in Texas, or How We Rocketed from Abysmal to Pretty Damn Good in Just Thirty Years. Texas schools were, for many years, like everything else that involves public money in this state: just awful. Texas ranked forty-ninth out of fifty states for so long in so many areas we came to believe the entire function of Mississippi was to prevent us from being last. The sole exception is highways: Texas has always built Cadillac highways. One of our unofficial state mottos is "Mississippi with Good Roads." This would be more forgivable if Texas were as poor as Mississippi, but in fact it's a remarkably wealthy state: Texas is the eleventh-largest economy in the world.

In 1968 the state was hauled into federal court by citizens of the extremely poor Edgewood school district in San Antonio over the gross inequities in the way rich kids and poor kids were educated in Texas. The case got to the U.S. Supreme Court in 1973, but the district lost on a 5–4 vote. The case was filed again in state court in 1984, finally tried in 1987, and Edgewood won at last. As a result of that victory, Governor Bill Clements had to sign a huge tax bill in 1989 to fund the agreement. For thirty years this case hung over state government; no matter where it was in the courts, it was apparent the state would have to equalize school funding somehow. The fight was always over how and by how much. The Legislature wrestled with it almost every session, trying to find some school-funding formula that would bring the poor districts up without taking away from the rich ones. The formula for state aid to public schools became so complex, the capitol press corps decided at one point in the eighties that it was understood by exactly three living human beings, none of whom could explain it.

Many are the fathers and mothers of education reform, but Governor Mark White, 1982–86, should get honorable mention. White had campaigned on higher wages for classroom teachers, but he couldn't get the '83 Lege to budge on it. Their message was clear: No more money for the schools unless the quality of education is improved, and there has to be some way to measure that. White had the unlikely notion of naming H. Ross Perot to head up a special blue-ribbon task force to figure out how to improve public schools. Perot may be slightly nutty on some subjects, but he's quite sound on education, a longtime interest of his, and of course, he brings phenomenal energy to any project. The Perot Commission held hearings all over Texas and raised dust wherever it went, a Texas twister of energy. One cynical axiom of Texas politics is that if it weren't for progressive bidnessmen, there wouldn't be any progressives at all in the state. One of Perot's greatest contributions was to preach to every bidness group in the state: If we don't fix the schools, your bidness will go to hell; we have to have educated workers. Bob Bullock was then state comptroller and understood the state's finances like few others; he and Perot figured out how to march the state toward equitable school financing over a period of several years so the system wouldn't be wrenched around all at once. And Perot took on the greatest power in all of Texas: football. The trouble with Texas schools, said Perot, is too much football. Pretty much the whole state flat fell down at hearing such heresy, bewildered as a goat on AstroTurf. The widespread consensus in Texas was that schools exist primarily to support football. Here Ross Perot up and proposed no-pass/no-play: If you don't pass all your courses in school, you can't play football. People were astounded, and it upset the coaches. In Texas politics, it is not wise to upset the coaches. White called a special session in 1984 to do nothing but the Perot reform package, known by its legislative moniker, H.B. 72. Damnedest fight you ever saw. With the possible exception of a redistricting battle, an education-reform effort is the single most depressing display of naked self-interest in the pantheon of spectator sports. The teacher groups fought for teacher interests, the administrators fought for administrator interests, the school boards fought for the schools boards, and not a single soul gave a damn about the kids. Tom Luce, a civilized Republican from Dallas and a real gentleman, was Perot's point man on the bill. He went in to see one state rep and gave a noble and inspiring pitch, ending with the observation that the future of Texas children would be determined by the quality of their education. The rep looked up and inquired, "The little fuckers have a PAC?"

To top it all was the absurdity of expecting the Legislature to fix all this. Whenever you hear a politician carry on about what a mess the schools are, be aware that you are looking at the culprit. The main reason the schools are a mess is because of the politicians. In Texas, the Lege had mandated over the years, among many other ludicrous and useless diversions, that the schools teach appreciation of capitalism, kindness to birds in the nest, and intelligent patriotism. To politicians, a state mandate to the schools was like a resolution. Any passing political fad or pea-brained notion of a powerful legislator got encoded as a state mandate to the schools; they multiplied like barnacles. Representative Paul Sadler, chair of the House Education Committee since 1995, says he still has to kill about 350 of these bills every session. Then the pols work themselves into a fine state of indignation over why the schools don't work.

During the fight over H.B. 72, Perot actually hired his own lobbyists to help the reforms along. Our then–lieutenant governor, the unusually civilized Bill Hobby, literally threw the teachers' lobbyists out of his office and wouldn't let them back in. At long last, almost all of the reforms recommended by the Perot Commission were enacted into law. Some legislators were defeated at the polls by angry football fans. Most experts agree the single most important step Texas took during the long process of reform was mandating smaller class sizes in the lower grades and emphasizing early education. Class size K through 4 is now limited to twenty-two pupils, and after years of effort we are close to funding full-day kindergarten statewide and are even working on prekindergarten programs. If you are looking for just one explanation for why Texas school scores have gone up so dramatically, that's the best pick, along with finally spending as much money on minority kids as we do on Anglo kids—the improvement in minority scores just blows away educators in other states. In a study done in the South Texas school district of Brownsville from 1975 to 1977, the smallest class was forty-six kids, and many classes had more than fifty. Mandating smaller class sizes and giving the poor districts enough money to implement that are the critical factors.

But before the equalization measures in H.B. 72 could be fully implemented, the state went broke. The oil bidness was gone to hell, state revenues dried up, and we didn't have the money to fix the schools.

The Edgewood decision in 1989 not only forced a tax

increase but was also followed by Son of Edgewood and Grandson of Edgewood, decisions demanding further refinements in the equalization system. After the '91 regular legislative session, four special sessions had to be called to deal with it all. They tried one Band-Aid after another in an effort to fix it. The key players during these years were Ernestine Glossbrenner, a teacher from Alice and chair of House Education,* and Senator Carl Parker, a particularly unpolished gem from Port Arthur, chair of Senate Education. One of Parker's great contributions was his consoling observation, "If you took all the fools out of the Legislature, it wouldn't be a representative body anymore." Representative Bill Haley of Center, who hid his sophistication behind an aggravated East Texas accent, also did heavy lifting. "This deal's been saucered and blowed," he once announced in tones that made Jethro Bodine sound like an Oxford graduate. Representative Paul Colbert of Houston, from his position on the Appropriations Committee, had a major hand in reshaping school finance; Colbert became such a walking encyclopedia on school finance that members used him as though he were Big Blue, the IBM computer. (He might be smarter than Blue.) From beginning to end, there were no major Republican players on education reform; Bush is not even entitled to credit by party affiliation. These same players also helped develop the accountability system.

By 1993, with Richards as governor and Representative Libby Linebarger as chair of House Education, school equalization was upon us once more. Even after adding

*Representative Glossbrenner is a heavy woman: for several years she gamely stood at the front mike and sang on *sine die* night, the last night of the session, to fit the saying "It's not over till the fat lady sings." This example of Texas legislative humor was mercifully scuttled when the other women in the House insisted on joining her.

more revenue to the pot, the only solution was to take some away from the rich districts and give it to the poor districts. One of the most consistent reactions in politics is the unholy uproar that follows whenever you try to take away special privileges. Makes no difference how obvious the unfairness is, those who have been favored over others by the system invariably feel entitled to that favoritism. It is theirs by right, by heritage, tradition, and divine providence, and if you try to take it away, you are in for the fight of your life. The underprivileged in this country can still raise a fair political stink on occasion, but it is nothing compared with the titanic stench that erupts when the overprivileged are invited onto a level playing field. The Robin Hood bill, which would have achieved some rough parity between the school districts of Texas, passed the Lege with no more difficulty than a mouse would have giving birth to a camel. It then went to the voters as a referendum in the form of three school-finance proposals. Richards worked hard to get it passed, running a high-profile campaign, but it lost overwhelmingly. It was denounced in some papers as "socialism." And again, some courageous members who voted for it were later punished at the polls. The Lege then whipped out a new version of Robin Hood, actually more radical than that rejected by the voters. This one presented the rich districts with a group of choices about how to give up their extra wealth. The courts kindly held that this version met Edgewood's requirements and did not require a referendum.

H.B. 72, particularly sticking with smaller class sizes year after year, plus early-childhood education programs plus equalizing school funding, is the real explanation for why school test scores, especially among minority students, are going up so noticeably. Having a system of testing and accountability makes the public much happier with the schools. For those who fought and died upon the field of the Robin Hood bill, nothing chaps them more than hearing George W. Bush claim the credit for improved test scores, especially among minority students. The better scores predate Bush's first campaign, as does the system of accountability from the schools. Those who believe in the karmic what-goes-around-comes-around will be amused to learn that by 1999 many of those same oil-rich districts that opposed the Robin Hood bill to the last ounce of their energy were themselves broke in yet another oil bust and demanding increased state aid under the Robin Hood formula.

"Almost everything he [Bush] claims credit for was done before he came in," says Representative Paul Sadler, chair of the House Education Committee. "The scores have been going up and the number who failed TAAS going down at the same steady rate since before Bush was elected." Still, some progress has been made since '95, and Bush has always been helpful and sometimes instrumental, as Sadler is the first to admit. In the 1995 session the major project was rewriting the education code, mostly to get rid of the endless state mandates, something every chair going back to Wilhelmina Delco in the 1970s has wanted to do.

Sadler, currently acknowledged as the Lege's scholar of schools, says solemnly, "Reform of education in Texas is very dangerous." He couldn't get Ann Richards to tackle the code—she said she wouldn't waste her political capital on it—but W. Bush could and did. Sadler also points out that educational changes are generational changes; it takes that long to see how they finally work out. But getting rid of the endless mandates and the TEA's leaden rules and regs is, so far, an easy net plus.

By 1997, the money problem was back. If Bob Bullock were still here to explain what's wrong with Texas finances, he would tell you that we have a twenty-first-century economy and a nineteenth-century tax structure. In Texas, taxes are still based on the land and the wealth that comes from the land—farming, ranching, rice, oil. But the wealth of the state is in banking, insurance, high tech, chemicals, airlines, NASA, and so forth. A homely analogy of which he was fond is the three-legged stool. In most states, government financing rests on a three-legged stool—property tax, sales tax, and income tax. In Texas, the stool has only two legs. So many politicians for so long have gotten elected by promising that Texas will have an income tax only over their cold dead bodies that this is now ingrained in the political culture. As a result, of course, we have the third most regressive tax structure in the country; in fact, looked at as a financial entity, the state of Texas is a system of income redistribution that takes from the poor and gives to the rich. Texas doesn't even have a corporate income tax as such, although Bullock managed to finagle through the Lege something called a corporate franchise tax, which more or less functions as the same thing.

Sadler explains, "We missed the opportunity in '93 to fix a horribly unfair system. Bullock always said the only chance we have to change it is when we have to shut down the schools. Well, we were there in '93, and we could have taken on the tax system, but Richards wouldn't do it. The Robin Hood bill was just a Band-Aid. I told the speaker, 'Pete, this bill is constitutional today, but at most you have five years [before the courts intervene].' And it would have crashed by now except we have this surplus from the good economy so we've been able to funnel more and more money into the system to keep it afloat."

Bush began the '97 session by proposing a major property-tax cut, but you can't touch property taxes without messing up school funding. So Pete Laney kicked Bush's tax proposal over to a select committee of four of the most powerful chairmen in the House, and he put Paul Sadler of Education in charge. One hundred days and three hundred witnesses later, out came a tax bill bearing no resemblance to the governor's original proposal.

The governor got his $1 billion in property-tax relief onto the House floor for debate. But the House Select Committee made sure public-education funding was not put at risk. They completely reworked the governor's tax plan, spreading the burden of taxation and for the first time bringing in limited partnerships (read: law firms and doctors), which were not taxed previously because they are not corporations. They also extended the sales tax to service businesses. And the governor stayed right on board. In short, they shifted $12 billion in taxes off of some shoulders and onto others, making the whole system much fairer: not increasing the sales tax but broadening it, mostly by closing one loophole after another. (Over the years, lobbyists have managed to insert so many loopholes in the sales tax, it looks like a doily. The majority of Texas tax law has been written by lobbyists.)

Whenever the Lege threatens to do any serious tax reform, a peculiar sound can be heard all over the state: It's all those corporate jets in Houston, Dallas, Midland, and Tyler, firing up simultaneously to head for Austin and stop this commie nonsense. What a fight. In addition to the usual legions of corporate lobbyists, the giant law firms like Vinson & Elkins in Houston and Akin Gump in Dallas were riled up; senior partners descended on the capitol in droves to oppose the tax on partnerships. CEOs from Fortune 500

companies showed up and threatened to shut down their
Texas operations if the Lege approved the corporate domi-
cile tax, which would reach into the pockets of companies
doing business in Texas but paying taxes only in Delaware.
The doctors were up in arms. Accountants could calculate
the new tax they would pay on their limited partnerships.
Even the barbers were in a snit, worried that a tax on
services would make haircuts unfashionable.

During a similar tax fight in the early seventies, Representative Jumbo Ben Atwell of Dallas, who was a charac-
ter even by the standards of the Lege, was chairman of Ways
and Means and had to carry a tax bill. The first speaker at
the back mike said, "Jumbo, no one in history has ever had
it written on his tombstone that he passed a tax bill." Atwell
said, "Well, I will." And he did: He rests today in the Texas
State Cemetery under a handsome slab of pink granite in the
shape of Texas. On it are carved Jumbo's name, dates, and
LAWYER—LEGISLATOR—AUTHOR OF A TAX BILL.

They needed Jumbo in the '97 fight. House Republicans,
who vote against anything resembling taxation, began to
run from their governor. The state Republican Party chairman bought ads in East Texas newspapers attacking Bush's
tax bill. Democrats showed up for floor debate wearing
lapel stickers that read FIFTY DS—FIFTY RS, serving notice
that they would not stick their necks out to vote for the bill
unless at least fifty Republicans joined them. And on the first
day of floor debate, the black and Mexican-American cau-
cuses walked off the floor.

After three days of arm-twisting and acrimony, the bill
passed the House in a late-night vote, forty house Republicans joining seventy-four Democrats. The governor strode
out onto the floor, first-naming his way through the pack of

representatives who had stayed with the bill. As reporters gathered around for a "gang bang"—an impromptu press conference—an aide told Bush the Texas Rangers had won their game. "Well, the Rangers won too," Bush said, beaming to reporters.

The Democrats were on board, the governor, leader of the Republicans, was on board; on paper, they should have won. But the lobby had just started to turn the screws in the Senate. Pauken, Bush's old political enemy, then chair of the Republican Party, accused the governor of supporting "hundreds of tax increases," that being the closing of the loopholes. True, some special interests would have paid more, but the net effect was a wash, no additional revenue to the state, just fairer. Almost none of the loopholes involve the general public. An example would be, say, an exemption on an industrial solvent used only by plastics makers. Bush worked like a Trojan. It came down to an end-of-session Friday-night vote, and Bush couldn't hold the Republicans. Bullock couldn't hold them; even Bill Ratliff, the Republican Bullock had named chair of Senate Education, wouldn't go along. "I love you like a brother, Governor," said Ratliff, "but I won't do it." Sadler swears Ratliff never even read the bill, just took the lobby's word for what was in it. He also thinks Ratliff never showed the senators the result of the district runs—how the changes would affect their school districts.

Ratliff today says that he had said from the start of the session that he would back only $1 billion in tax shifts, and when Bush and Bullock came to him with $1.5 billion, he just said no. He recalls heavy pressure by the governor and lieutenant governor but says he wasn't affected by it.

Bullock had lost leverage because the Senate had already

passed the finance bill before the vote on the tax bill, so he couldn't threaten to cut off their junior colleges (one of his favorite tactics). Bush and Bullock tried to turn it all day Saturday: they met one-on-one, they turned every screw they could find, they called all the senators in for a come-to-Jesus session. A great deal of cussing occurred. But the lobby won. The lobby and the fear of being accused of having "increased taxes" even though there was no overall tax increase. Incidentally, Steve Forbes is now using the old Pauken charge that Bush supported "hundreds of tax increases."

Sadler said philosophically, "We lost because there wasn't a crisis; we weren't about to have to shut down the schools." Players in both parties say Bush was willing to put it all on the line for education in both '95 and '97. But by the '99 session, the presidential bid was starting to eat him up. He spent part of every day raising money and part of every day being taught by various experts not to call the Timorese "Timorians." He was not much of a player and, as described earlier, pretty much abandoned his own voucher initiative.

We're Number One:
Bush and Criminal Justice

*Texas' bloodthirsty criminal justice officials. . . . Texas, where
liberals are required to carry visas and compassion is virtually
illegal. . . . A state perfectly willing to execute the retarded
and railroad the innocent . . . by far the most backward state
in the nation when it comes to capital punishment. . . .
Texas has a fetish for capital punishment.*
—Bob Herbert, *The New York Times*

Maybe he was a little overexcited about the state of criminal justice in Texas. But then, we've earned it. You want tough on crime? We're number one. You want a fair trial? There could be a problem. Our reputation is worldwide, indisputable.

☆ Texas has approximately 147,000 people in its state prisons, the largest prison system on the planet Earth. Counting those in the state's jails and on parole, there are 545,000 people in the system.

☆ For every 100,000 adult Texans, 700 of them are in prison. The national average is 452 per 100,000 population.

☆ On any given day, we have about 450 people on death row. Since the U.S. Supreme Court lifted its four-year moratorium on executions in 1976, Texas has killed 138 people, more than one third of all the executions in the country. Bush himself had signed 100 death warrants by the fall of 1999, more than any previous governor.

☆ Only once in the past seventeen years has the Texas Board of Pardons and Paroles, appointed by the governor, recommended that a death sentence be commuted. The perp was the serial liar Henry Lee Lucas, who confessed to more than 120 murders and was charged with 35 before anyone in Texas had the mother wit to wonder if he was lying. He is now believed to be guilty of one or perhaps two murders. The state of Texas, with no difficulty at all, managed to give Lucas the death penalty for a murder committed while Lucas was in another state entirely. Oops.

☆ We have executed people who are hopelessly mentally ill, people who are profoundly retarded, and people who are innocent—and that is all well-known fact.

☆ Should you draw the death penalty in this state, you have thirty days to find any evidence that would exculpate you. If no new evidence is found or someone else confesses on day thirty-one, you are SOL.

George W. Bush's record over five and half years is to have made this draconian system even worse; at every single turn where he could have done something to make the system less savagely punitive, he went out of his way to do the opposite.

While we have no interest in Bush's "youthful indiscretions," we do think it is fair to call him on his oft-repeated claim that he has learned from his mistakes. What did he learn? Where is the evidence that he learned anything at all? Twenty-one percent of the people in Texas prisons are there on drug-related charges. Assume George W. Bush as a young man smoked marijuana. There are now 7,400 people in Texas state prisons on marijuana charges,* and 3,100 of them are there for possession only. According to the U.S. Bureau of Justice Statistics, there are at least 5,700 more in Texas county jails for possession of marijuana only. That's at least 8,800 people doing time for doing exactly what George W. Bush might have done. If you assume George W. Bush used cocaine as a young man, there are at least 8,300 in Texas prisons for possession only. The case of Melinda George, who was sentenced to ninety-nine years in prison for possession of one tenth of a gram of cocaine, is merely the most infamous of the Texas coke cases.** According to the Texas Department of Public Safety, 28,158 people were arrested in the state last year for possession of cocaine.

Because he was a rich white kid with an important daddy, Bush's chances of going to prison for drug use were nil. Yet there is no recognition anywhere in his record of "There but for the grace of God go I." In fact, to the contrary, Bush has acted to make sure that poor folks have even less access to justice in the system.

He vetoed a bill in the summer of '99 that would have required each county to set up a system—any kind of system— for appointing attorneys to represent indigent defendants. We believe Texas is the only state in the country with no system at all for meeting the constitutional requirement that indigent defendants be provided counsel. Instead, each district judge is in charge of appointing counsel for those defendants before him or her. And each judge can do this by whatever

*From statistics compiled by the Justice Department's Bureau of Justice Statistics and the Marijuana Project.
**Ms. George had hacked off her jury by failing to show for one court appearance, an omission that cost her heavily.

means His Honor chooses, including the traditional brother-in-law merit system.

Just for starters, district judges are elected, which means they are sensitive to campaign contributors. Surprisingly, 25 percent of Texas' district judges admitted in a state bar poll that campaign contributions do affect their appointment decisions. We have one well-documented case where the lawyer slept through the testimony in his client's case, which ended with a death sentence. In another, the appointed attorney met his client for the first time during jury selection and refused to consider the client's alibi, which was that he was incarcerated in another county at the time of the crime. This citizen spent five years behind bars before a federal judge threw the case out. And in many, many cases defendants have spent months in jail before they were even assigned a lawyer.

In response to these and many more documented abuses, the Legislature overwhelmingly passed and sent to Governor Bush the bill requiring counties to have a system that would provide a lawyer for an indigent client within twenty days of requesting one. Actually, most Texas judges already meet that requirement, but there are far too many exceptions. People spend literally months in jail without a lawyer. The bill had the support of a wide range of legal scholars, county officials, defense attorneys—in fact, everybody except the district judges, long accustomed to total, personal power over indigent defendants who appear before them.

Bush caved to the district judges and vetoed the bill, saying it would be "a drastic change in the way indigent criminal defendants are assigned counsel." Drastic? Twenty days? In most of the country, defendants must have a lawyer within seventy-two hours.

Bush also came out against a bill that would have pro-

hibited the use of the death penalty against profoundly retarded criminals; instead, a capital murderer found to be
retarded would have been sentenced to life in prison without
parole. In 1989 the U.S. Supreme Court ruled that although
mental retardation could constitute a mitigating circum-
stance in a death-penalty case, it would be up to the states to
legislate to that effect. Since then, twelve of the states that
have the death penalty have prohibited execution of the
mentally retarded and Congress has banned it in federal
cases. You've met Labrador retrievers brighter than some of
the people Texas executes.

Bush's sole explanation for his position was "I like the
law the way it is right now." Texans love the death penalty,
but a 1998 Texas Poll shows 73 percent of those in the state
are opposed to executing the retarded. Nationally, two-
thirds of those polled on the question support a ban on the
death penalty for mentally retarded murderers. There wasn't
even a political percentage in Bush's stand.

One retardate thought he had been sentenced to death
because he didn't know how to read and kept trying desperately to learn while he was in prison, thinking it would
save him. Another kept asking his legal-aid lawyer what
he should wear to his funeral, under the impression that he
would be there for it. And there is a possibly apocryphal
story—we were not able to confirm it—about a retarded in-
mate who asked for pudding for dessert with his last supper.
When guards asked why he hadn't eaten the pudding, he
said he was saving it for later.

The bill Bush opposed set retardation at an IQ of less than
65, even though 70 is the national norm; the law would not
have applied to those currently on death row. The Republican-
dominated Senate passed the bill, but House members were

nervous about Bush's stated opposition and let it die without action, so he didn't have to veto it after all.

It was especially puzzling, since the bill would have been a perfect showcase for "compassionate conservatism"—it had broad popular support, affected very few people, and cost nothing.

Whether or not Bush used drugs in the late 1960s and early 1970s, Texas then had the harshest drug laws in the nation: First-offense possession of any amount of marijuana was a two-to-life felony. You may need to read that again: two years to life in prison for first-offense possession of any amount of marijuana. The most notable victim of that law was a young black activist from Houston, Lee Otis Johnson, who got thirty years for passing a joint (not smoking it or selling it, passing it) in the presence of an undercover cop.* This law made no observable difference to an entire generation of young Texans, who got stoned just as often as young people anywhere else in the country. It was finally changed in August 1973, after even our Legislature had to acknowledge it was making no difference. Oddly enough, the state of New York then adopted the same ridiculously stringent drug laws the state of Texas had just dropped—as usual, not because it made any sense, but because the then-governor,

---

*Johnson, who had led civil rights demonstrations at Texas Southern University, was clearly the target of a setup by the Houston Police Department, which in those days had Klan members in its headquarters. For years he was the most famous political prisoner in Texas. In 1968, when Governor Preston Smith made a campaign speech at the University of Houston, the students chanted, "Free Lee Otis! Free Lee Otis!" so loudly that Smith was unable to finish the speech. Next day, all the state's papers were outraged over the discourtesy to the governor. Smith himself, when asked about the Free Lee Otis demo, replied, "Oh! Is that what they was yellin'? I thought they was sayin' 'Frijoles, frijoles.' I couldn't figure out what they had against frijoles. I think that's some kind of dried bean." Johnson was eventually released, but by then his experiences had soured him: he committed another crime and went back in stir.

Nelson Rockefeller, wanted to build a record for being Tuff on Crime.

So Bush, who presumably knows from personal experience that harsh laws do not deter drug use, finally gets to be governor himself, and what does he do? Supports tougher drug laws. In 1997 Bush signed a law making the penalties for possession of less than one gram of cocaine even harsher. Before he signed that law, state sentencing guidelines required that a judge give mandatory probation in such a case; the new law allows judges to sentence those in possession of less than one gram of cocaine to jail. In 1995 Bush signed a bill increasing the punishment for anyone selling or possessing drugs within one thousand feet of a school or a school bus.

Again, the issue here is what Bush learned. Time and time and time again he has said the mistakes he made are not important, all that matters is that he learned from those mistakes. What did he learn?

When Ann Richards left office, Texas had just started on one of the most ambitious programs in the country to treat drug and alcohol addiction among prisoners. This has long been the great goal of those who work with addictive disease: to get treatment in the prisons, where it is so demonstrably needed. The program was the joint legacy of Richards and Lieutenant Governor Bob Bullock, both recovering alcoholics.* According to the Texas Department of Criminal Justice's own figures—taken from academic, psychological, and medical tests given all entering prisoners—

*Though Bullock and Richards later fell out with one another for complicated reasons, Bullock never forgot that when he returned to Austin at two in the morning after a month at "whiskey school" in California, sober for the first time in years and scared to death he would drink again, there was one person at the airport to meet him—Ann Richards.

80 to 85 percent of those in Texas prisons have a history of drug or alcohol abuse. The figure is higher for women. "Substance-abuse problem" is defined as having abused drugs at the time of the crime or within the previous thirty days.

Richards and Bullock began the effort to fund significant drug-rehabilitation programs in the prisons in 1991. The Lege agreed to drug rehab for fourteen thousand prisoners as soon as the TDCJ had enough beds for all prisoners. This was during the enormous prison-building spree; the state went from 41,000 beds in 1989 to 150,000, including 5,000 for youth offenders. In '91 the Lege approved the first billion-dollar bond issue for prison building. All this took place, of course, because the state was under court order; federal judge William Wayne Justice of the Eastern District had by then declared overcrowding in state prisons so severe it amounted to unconstitutionally cruel and unusual punishment. Every summer the prisoners, crammed together practically on top of one another in the suffocating East Texas heat, would have mini-riots. So, the number of prison beds tripled during Richards' administration, at a cost of $1.7 billion. Meanwhile, in order to meet the court order on overcrowding, the state's prisoners were kept longer in the county jails, and the jails backed up and overflowed, so the counties sued the state, which then had to pay a huge daily fine. It was a mess.

By 1993, TDCJ had built some new beds and was ready to start a drug-treatment program; the Lege then authorized another billion in bonds for even more beds. According to the studies and experts consulted when Texas first set up its in-prison substance-abuse program, one critical element is the timing. Putting the treatment near the end of a prisoner's sentence maximizes the benefit, since the goal is for the prisoner to carry the techniques of restraint into the real world. Follow-up is equally critical for the same reason.

Of the several types of drug treatment and counseling now in use, the best option seems to be a therapeutic community, modeled after Phoenix House and similar efforts. Richards' staff felt strongly that the program should not be administered by the TDCJ, which still tends to produce old-style Texas wardens. The appropriation for the physical plant went through the TDCJ, but the treatment program itself was funded through the Texas Commission on Alcohol and Drug Abuse (called TCADA, an acronym we can almost pronounce). Because some legislators were interested in "front-door" programs—for prisoners just coming into the system—rather than the "back-door" approach most experts recommend, additional money was put into those beds. Carol Vance, a Richards appointee, former D.A. in Houston, and devout Christian, also had a voice in the program, and he wanted Christian-based and values-based rehab programs. These are short-term, front-end programs with no aftercare, and they are now part of the plea-bargaining system: Cop down to a lesser charge, do six months in a prison rehab program, and you're out.

In the '94 campaign, Bush specifically campaigned against the drug treatment program, vowing to take $25 million out of it to incarcerate more juveniles. The original program has been pretty much bastardized; mostly because nobody is paying much attention to it, it has no champions. Even Bullock didn't try to save it, feeling it was "Ann's deal" and he was sore at her. In the '95 session, Representative Rob Junell got a hard-on against the folks at TCADA for allegedly wasting money, so he took the program away from them and put it under TDCJ, in whose less-than-tender care it has since resided. Bottom line: At the end of '94 Texas had 4,261 beds for in-prison, back-door, therapeutic-community treatment with follow-up, and there were another 2,000 on line. In late 1999 there are 5,300 beds available for all the drug-treatment programs, but only 800 are for the back-door beds originally envisioned. The state has relied on experts who say most of the prisoners with addictions are in denial so treatment would be a waste of money. (Treatment, of course, is designed to break through denial.) Another problem is that the back-door program in TDCJ depends on the parole board first deciding to release a con, and the parole board just doesn't do much paroling.

It is especially tragic that Texas let this opportunity slip away, since more and more studies of successful programs in other states show an astonishing payoff. The federal Bureau of Prisons says inmates who have received treatment are 73 percent less likely to be rearrested in the first six months after release. A 1997 Rand Corporation study says treatment reduces about ten times more serious crime than conventional law enforcement does and fifteen times more than mandatory minimums. A state of California study shows that every dollar spent on treatment saves seven dollars in reduced hospital admissions and law-enforcement costs.

Bush's hard-liner attitude toward anyone in prison includes some notorious cases. In 1985 Kevin James Byrd, a twenty-two-year-old black Houstonian, was convicted of brutally raping a pregnant woman. He was convicted on the word of the victim, who saw him in a grocery store four months after the crime and identified him as her rapist. This was four years before Houston courts began allowing DNA evidence in trials. Byrd spent twelve years in prison, always maintaining his innocence. An old friend finally gave him some financial help so he could pay for DNA tests, which proved it was not his semen in the victim.

Harris County district attorney Johnny Holmes, a Republican law-'n'-order man to the bone, and the district judge in the case and even all eighteen members of the Board of Pardons and Paroles recommended that Bush pardon Kevin Byrd. He refused to do it. This refusal caused a flap in the media, so Bush's aides announced that the governor wanted "all other legal remedies exhausted." This meant Byrd had to raise money to get his case through the state's appellate courts, even though Holmes made it clear he thought Byrd was innocent and had no intention of retrying him, even if the appeals court granted a new trial. Byrd eventually got his pardon, but only after he had spent more time and more money jumping through legal hoops.

Texas' questionable system of pardons came under national scrutiny in 1998 in the case of Karla Faye Tucker. Fifteen years earlier Tucker, then a twenty-three-year-old prostitute and drug addict, and her boyfriend had bludgeoned two people to death with a pickax. During her years in prison, she became a born-again Christian and began a prison ministry that eventually included extensive correspondence with people in prison in other states and other countries, as well as many, many in Texas. She admitted her crime and expressed remorse. She even won over Pat Robertson, head of the Christian Coalition, who pleaded with Bush to spare her life. If he did not, said Robertson, he was "a man of no mercy."

Tucker's attorney asked that the death penalty be commuted to life in prison without parole, on the grounds that she had demonstrated repentance and rehabilitation. Those familiar with the state's death row politics thought she had a chance. Not as a woman, no one was making that plea; nor as a born-again Christian—Texas prisoners often find God, and it has never yet been held grounds for commuting the death sentence. However, using the old Christian distinction between faith and works—of which Governor Bush is presumably aware—Tucker had not just faith but works to display, years of work, an enormous volume of correspondence.

The Board of Pardons and Paroles never even met to consider Tucker's request for commutation. They never met with her or her attorney, never voted in public, and never explained their reasons for turning her down. And this is standard operating procedure in Texas. The board has no guidelines for when to recommend commutation; it carries out all its decisions in secret, not even required to meet in public on death-penalty cases, so the public has no way of knowing why the board does what it does. Nor does anyone outside the system know what is in a prisoner's file, on which the board bases its decision. Defense attorneys claim prison records and prisoner files often contain terrible misinformation, another reason to make the hearings public.

In September 1999, a profile of Bush in *Talk* magazine appeared and contained this passage by reporter Tucker Carlson:

In the weeks before the execution, Bush says, Bianca Jagger and a number of other protesters came to Austin to demand clemency for Tucker. "Did you meet with any of them?" I ask.

Bush whips around and stares at me. "No, I didn't meet

with any of them," he snaps, as though I've just asked the dumbest question ever posed. "I didn't meet with Larry King either when he came down for it. I watched his interview with her, though. He asked her real difficult questions, like, 'What would you say to Governor Bush?' "

"What was her answer?" I wonder.

"Please," Bush whimpers, his lips pursed in mock desperation, "don't kill me."

I must look shocked—ridiculing the pleas of a condemned prisoner who has since been executed seems odd and cruel, even for someone as militantly anti-crime as Bush—because he immediately stops smirking.

Carlson also reports that the exchange Bush mimicked never took place during the King interview. When the *Talk* article appeared, the Bush campaign issued a statement saying Carlson had misunderstood Bush. Carlson replied in turn that he did not misunderstand.

A state official who spent time with Bush the day Tucker was to be executed says Bush seemed genuinely troubled over it and spent a long time in private conversation talking about the whole issue of capital punishment. At a guess, his being flip about it with Carlson was a defensive reaction. But we find no evidence Bush has been troubled by the other ninety-nine executions he could have stopped.

Shortly after Tucker's execution in February of '98, two other convicted killers facing execution challenged the secretive clemency process in federal court. Judge Sam Sparks ruled that the system was legal but strongly deplored it from the bench, stating, "Even though this Board represents the public, there is nothing—absolutely no way the public, even the governor, can know the reason for their vote without asking each one of them. I find that appalling. A flip of the coin would be more merciful than these votes, and [the procedure] is extremely poor and certainly minimal."

So in 1999, Representative Elliott Naishtat introduced a modest bill to improve the system, requiring the board to hold a public hearing if a prisoner under death sentence requested commutation to imprisonment. The board was not required to vote in public, nor were any guidelines suggested. The prisoner or his attorney would be permitted to appear, and later, after its determination, the board would be required to give a reason for its decision.

The bill caused a great hue and cry of opposition from the governor's office. Bush said since a federal judge had found the system constitutional, he saw nothing wrong with its secrecy. He said public hearings would cause people to "rant and rave" and get all emotional. The bill died.

When Bush ran for governor in 1994 he made a big issue of what appeared to be an increase in juvenile crime. He would announce: "It's always been normal, when a child turns into a criminal, to say that it's our fault—society's fault. Well, under George W. Bush, it's your fault. You're going to get locked up because we aren't going to have any more guilt-ridden thought that says we are somehow responsible." So in his first session, Bush was part of a big push to change the juvenile-justice code. It was completely rewritten, and the population of the state's juvenile prisons has since tripled. Hal Gaither, a Bush adviser and Dallas juvenile-court judge who describes himself as "the most conservative man in Texas," told *The New York Times*, "If George W. Bush can do for the United States what he has done for Texas, no one can lick his boots."

If you think the main purpose of a juvenile-justice system should be punishment, by all means, lick Bush's boots.

The trouble with Texas as the National Laboratory for Bad Government is that we never throw away an old bad idea. The poor man from the *Times* identified "protecting the best interest of the child" as "the historical role" of the juvenile-justice system. Not in this state. The old Texas Youth Commission was so notoriously punitive it finally came under the scrutiny of Judge Justice, long before the adult prisons did. On August 31, 1973, Justice issued a restraining order that is among the most hideous reading in the annals of American law. In it, the Youth Commission is enjoined from beating, gassing, racking, encouraging homosexual rape, denying medical care, and torturing kids in reform school in a specified list of ways that make you want to vomit just reading them. Getting tough on youth crime a new idea? Not in this state. We already tried it. It didn't work. For years, the single highest predictor of who wound up in adult prisons in Texas was who had done time as a juvenile; we were running factories making adult criminals. That's changing—the predictor, not the system. In a depressing portent of things to come, corrections systems are now finding that the single greatest predictor of who winds up in prison is having a father who did time in prison.

Political Free Speech:
Bush and Campaign Finance

*It was an amazing thing to watch. While [Governor Bush]
was doing his legislative work, he has sat down and
had lunch with people from around the country—
basically letting the money people come to him.*
—A Republican Party fund-raiser
quoted in *The New York Times*

"Normally it's like crawling over broken glass to get
clients to cough up campaign donations," an Austin lobbyist said. "But with Bush, for the first time, we've got clients
calling me wanting to know how and where to send money.
Some of them have gotten downright irritated with me if I
couldn't give them all the details immediately."

The governor's presidential-campaign fund-raising is so
successful that it threatens representative democracy as we
practice it in Texas. "It's just draining away all the money
needed for other races," said a lobbyist worried about how
he'll get anything passed in the next session if his clients
can't write checks to committee chairs and incumbents.

You can't blame the governor for success in a system that
is so flush with campaign funding that nobody bothers to
steal elections anymore. Texas' most famous political tradi-

tion is lost. No need for anything like the famous ballot box from Precinct Thirteen in Duval County. Box Thirteen gave 425 votes to Lyndon Johnson and 2 votes to his opponent, providing Johnson the 89 votes he needed to defeat Coke Stevenson in the U.S. Senate primary runoff in 1948. It was an odd ballot box: three days late with the last 200 voters registered in a distinctly different ink from that of the first 227. Johnson won that race because he outstole Stevenson.

These days elections are bought and paid for up front. It's what University of Massachusetts–Boston professor Tom Ferguson calls money-driven election campaigns—and nowhere is it practiced quite like it is in Texas. With the exception of Bob Bullock, whose fund-raising office kept photocopies of inappropriate responses to Bullock's direct-mail solicitations, no Texas politician has worked the fund-raising system as well as Bush has. With $41 million in two statewide races, Bush now holds the all-time Texas record. (Bullock contributed $25,000 of that.)

Much of Bush's money has been raised by Karl Rove, the brains behind the Bush gubernatorial and presidential campaigns—and the campaigns of Senators Phil Gramm, Kay Bailey Hutchison, the state's attorney general, and the chief justice of the Texas Supreme Court. Rove is the former chair of the national College Republicans, who got so turned on by politics that he never finished his degree.

Rove's 1993 internal campaign memo ordering Bush's gubernatorial campaign staff to "limit GWB's public appearance" could have been the outline for Bush's spring '99 Yellow Rose Garden Campaign. Rove kept flying in policy experts to home-school his candidate, teaching him, among other things, that Kosovars are not called "Kosovarians." On one late-winter afternoon, as the press pack was leaving the capitol, the ornate iron gate behind the governor's mansion opened to make way for a black Suburban carrying a dyspeptic-looking George Shultz, who appeared to be carrying the weight of the world on his stomach—perhaps the result of a long foreign-policy tutorial.

While Bush avoided any discussion of public policy, Rove scheduled delegations of legislators and governors from around the country to fly in and endorse his undeclared candidate. At the same time, the Bush exploratory committee was raising money. It was brilliant, if a bit arrogant. When *Dallas Observer* reporter Miriam Rozen asked Rove why the press didn't challenge Bush when he refused to answer policy questions, a grinning Rove responded: "Because they were spellbound."

Rove also helped arrange the comings and goings of Republican funders flying into Austin for lunch with Bush. Rove, and Karl Rove & Associates, the company Bush insisted that Rove sell before the presidential campaign began, raised much of the money for Bush's two gubernatorial races. From the disclosure forms that fill seventeen boxes (another record) at the Texas Ethics Commission, you get some sense of how the money came in. Long lists of contributors who mailed in $10, $25, or $250 checks in response to mailings from Rove are punctuated by short lists of $5,000 and $10,000 and $25,000 checks written at fundraisers in Dallas, Houston, or Austin.

Texas is an urban state, but it's still the Wild West of campaign finance. No thousand-dollar limits on individual contributions like the stifling federal system. No need for soft-money schemes to beat the system. No huge PAC scene. The rules are simple. Any individual can make a contribution of any amount to any candidate or candidates. Once the contribution is reported by the candidate, it's legal. Corporations can't give, but corporate "good-government" PACs can. If political contributions are equal to "free speech," as the U.S. Supreme Court and Kentucky senator Mitch McConnell claim, then Texas is the First Amendment poster state.

We have imposed a few restrictions on "free speech." No longer can legislators engage in the unseemly practice of taking money during legislative sessions. We wouldn't have gotten that far without the generosity of East Texas chicken magnate Lonnie "Bo" Pilgrim. In 1989 the owner of Pilgrim's Pride Chicken walked onto the Senate floor during a committee hearing and handed $10,000 checks to senators wavering on a workers'-compensation reform designed to limit the rights of workers injured on the job. The press cried fowl and even by Texas standards the whole deal was so unseemly that senators had no choice but to say indignantly that those checks were going right back to Mr. Pilgrim. But even without the $10,000 incentive, the wavering senators were somehow persuaded to dismantle the workers'-comp system.

Pilgrim runs a vertically integrated chicken business that raises, kills, plucks, and trucks. His company has been cited for air and water pollution. Giving $10,000 checks to a half dozen senators ten years ago was not his only adventure in campaign funding. Texans for Public Justice, an Austin-based nonprofit research group, has studied Bush's major funders and found that at $125,000, Pilgrim ranks seventh on the list of big givers to Bush's two campaigns for governor. Pilgrim must have been pleased with his investment when the governor, who immediately on taking office demanded the resignations of the Democratic holdovers on the commission that monitors air and water quality. Bush's appointees eased enforcement standards, ended unannounced inspections, and paid far less attention to the quality of water in the state's streams.

There are bigger follow-the-money stories. The case of the grandfathered polluters (described in "Is the Air Cleaner?") is just one notable episode. If there is an Ozone Man (as Big George labeled Al Gore during the 1992 campaign) in the 2000 election, it's our governor. Much of the polluters' money arrived just when the public was pushing the Legislature to clean up the air. Dubya won the 1999 legislative fight to keep the grandfather loophole open after taking $263,698 in "ozone money" from industries contributing to the state's ozone smog in 1998, according to the Texas Campaign for the Environment.

The group also found that like airborne pollutants, political contributions are hard to contain. As the 1999 legislative session progressed, money from the same sources began to spill into Bush's presidential campaign. Individuals, law firms, and PACs connected to the state's top 100 grandfathered polluters contributed $316,300 to the exploratory committee during March, according to Texans for Public Justice—just as the Sierra Club and other green groups had persuaded a majority of legislators to pass a bill mandating modern environmental controls for all 850 grandfathered polluters. The Campaign for the Environment went to the Texas Natural Resources Conservation Commission and found that the 100 companies that donated the money had released 559,893 tons of grandfathered air pollution in the previous year—in the state with the most polluted air in the nation.

The $316,300 includes $138,900 from individual lawyers

with Vinson & Elkins, the law firm that represents Enron—
and Alcoa, a grandfathered facility and the state's largest-
volume air polluter. V&E does, after all, represent many
other clients. But do the math on the bundled $138,900—in
a federal system that caps individual contributions to a candidate at $1,000—and you come up with enough lawyers to
staff a good-size firm.

But $138,900 in contributions that fall under the $1,000-
per-person federal cap brings into high relief another
loophole—the bundling loophole in federal campaign funding. The grandfather loophole is arcane because it involves
engineering. The bundling loophole isn't. Any contributor
with a little imagination and a big family or business can
beat the $1,000 limit by funneling contributions through
Grandma, Grandpa, kids, cousins, business partners, or employees. (This is not to suggest that anyone at V&E wrote a
check for more than $1,000. Records show they didn't. But
the Bush fund-raisers who worked the law firm must have
written an effective letter.)

The really big winners in our wide-open campaign-
funding system, other than the governor, are the Texas Tort
Tycoons. All the big tort-reform funders have been tracked
down by Texans for Public Justice, another nonprofit pain
in the ass for corporate interests. In 1994 Bush ran on tort
reform, a series of laws that would make it more difficult for
individuals to sue business interests. In 1995 he declared tort
reform a legislative emergency. (Bush arrived as a decade of
tort reform was concluding but still early enough to use the
issue to raise big money.)

The emergency was little guys and plaintiffs' lawyers
teaming up to win large sums of money from corporate
defendants. "Clogging the courts, frivolous lawsuits, high

insurance rates, settlements or judgments that shut down businesses, bad business climate, and level playing field" were again the lobby buzz in the 1995 session. But for every story of an outrageous settlement or jury award handed down before 1995, there are hundreds of stories of plaintiffs who lost.

"We've always had tort reform in Amarillo," Jeff Blackburn observed. "In Amarillo we call it jury decisions." Blackburn—a chain-smoking courthouse-square lawyer who does everything but corporate defense law—knows where the bodies (and body parts) are hidden on the losing side of tort reform.

The tort reformers endlessly publicized high-dollar judgments like the draftsman whose surviving family members got more than $100 million out of a Houston oil company. The company required the man to clean his tools in benzene, a known carcinogen, which caused his death. Blackburn can tell you Amarillo-courtroom stories that would make you want to start your own tort-reform movement.

You will never see, for example, the headline JURY AWARDS MEXICAN-AMERICAN $30,000 AFTER SURGEON OPERATES ON WRONG FOOT. But $30,000 is the going rate for a working stiff's foot in Amarillo, where ten years ago local docs read a chart wrong and operated on the wrong foot of a patient. While the poor guy was still out, the surgeons went ahead and operated on the foot they were hired to repair. When the patient realized he'd lost the use of both feet, he sued for $1 million. The insurance company offered him $500,000, and the Amarillo lawyers watching from the sidelines knew he'd be wise to take it. But he believed his foot was worth more than that and worried that the inability to walk might make it hard to earn a living, so he looked to the jury for equity. He got $30,000. If there's no equity in Amarillo, there is at least an abiding respect for the consumer; the surgeon charged nothing for ruining the man's one good foot.

Tort reform has since changed the rules to make it drastically more difficult for plaintiffs. Blackburn can tell you about hundreds of workers seriously injured on IBP Corporation's Amarillo beef-packing production line. The old tort system never did them much good anyway, and they're having even less success in the courts today. And in a case involving a railway company, a Texas Supreme Court opinion written in 1996 by a Bush appointee to a vacant seat all but shuts workers out of the court system—removing their legal protection against employers who would fire them in retaliation for taking workplace injury complaints to a lawyer.

Texans for Public Justice identified $543,250 in tort-reform money Bush took in from just seven donors in the $75,000-plus category. Add to that $407,500 from the tort-reform PACs, and you are close to a million dollars, which buys a lot of reform. That's only the money they gave the governor. Totals paid to legislators and judges are harder to come by, but between 1993 and 1998, the two big tort-reform political action committees alone handed out more than $3.7 million to judges, legislators, the governor, and the lieutenant governor. Bush promised Texans in his 1999 State of the State address that he would "finish the work of tort reform." He also promised to work on tort reform if he is elected president. He has never promised to begin the work of campaign-finance reform.

Reporters at a March 2, 1999, press event at the mansion knew Dubya couldn't be serious when he said he didn't know how he would fare raising money with the $1,000 federal cap on individual donations. He had called the Texas press corps over to tell us he'd put together an exploratory committee, and as is usually the case, it was a friendly event. One reporter even asked the governor if he had any skeletons in his closet. He said no, and we were all relieved to have that out of the way. There were questions and blithe responses about the advice and consent of George and Barbara Bush, a short rap on the governor's record, and a few jokes about which members of his family would contribute to his campaign.

Within a month, the committee had raised $7.6 million, seven times what Lamar Alexander had amassed during his entire short-lived campaign. Until the end of the legislative session the governor appeared to avoid fund-raising and to honor the spirit of the Texas Election Code, which bans fund-raising for state elections while the Legislature is in session. Once the session ended, Bush brought in $37 million in six months—more than all eleven of his primary opponents combined raised in the same period—and one capitol insider's joke connected state rep Ron Wilson's attempt to keep Austin's old downtown airport open with the need to provide an easy turnaround for Bush donors.

It turns out that fund-raisers got plenty of use out of the old airport. In mid-May, Don Van Natta, Jr., of *The New York Times* reported that Bush had begun assembling a team of fund-raisers more than a year earlier, and that nearly five hundred donors had traveled to Austin in the several months before the May 16 story ran. "It was very stealthy and people did not realize it," one "longtime Republican fund-raiser" told Van Natta. "It was an amazing thing to watch. While he was doing his legislative work, he has sat down and had lunch with people from around the country—basically letting the money people come to him."

So Dubya's initial $7.6 million was raised not in a month but in a year and a month. And as the *Times* and the Campaign for the Environment have found, he was raising the money while the Lege was in session. Again, the Texas Election Code prohibits elected officials from raising funds for state campaigns while the Legislature is in session. But the statute doesn't cover fund-raising for federal elections.

Bush even holds the singular distinction of inventing a new category of fund-raising to be reformed. His Pioneers, each committed to raising $100,000, represent a level of contribution-bundling that renders the $1,000 individual federal cap meaningless. In fact, Bush has rendered almost all the post-Watergate campaign reform meaningless. In May Don Evans, Bush's big, movie-star-handsome, former oil-field partner from Midland, laid the groundwork for opting out of the primary spending cap—thereby refusing the federal funding that comes with spending limits. Evans said that if the campaign could raise $50 million, Bush would consider "going non-matching." But he warned that going from $37 to $50 million would not be easy. Then Evans, who is Bush's campaign finance director and Bush's appointee to the University of Texas Board of Regents, coordinated the raising of $50 million. Other candidates have turned down federal funding and limits on primary spending and get no federal funds. Steve Forbes will probably break the $33.5 million primary spending limit and get no federal funds. But Forbes is writing his own checks. Bush is the only candidate running on other people's money while choosing to ignore the most fundamental campaign-finance measures passed into law since the excesses of Watergate stunned the nation almost thirty years ago.

These big figures are "news" for the national press, but our campaign-finance system has weakened the gag reflex of most of us who write about politics in the Great State. So when a *Los Angeles Times* headline reads TEXAS CORPORATE INTERESTS FINANCED BULK OF BUSH RACES, we read on, assuming that when we finish we will have achieved that smug sense of satisfaction that comes with having told a story first. Bush's leading donors, *Times* reporter Alan C. Miller wrote, were oil and other large industrial companies trying to avert mandatory pollution controls (told you that); businesses seeking relief from expensive civil suits (wrote that story before); and conservatives advocating state-paid vouchers for students in private schools (no news there).

The numbers the *Times* produced are another story. Our hometown nonprofit, campaign-finance research groups soldier on, their resources always stretched thin. And we have no daily newspaper willing to invest the money required to do big analytical stories. So the numbers-crunching done by a newspaper with the resources and vision to take on such a project produced "Holy shit!" reactions that are still reverberating through the Texas press corps and the offices of the nonprofits who thought they knew how much money Bush was getting, and who was giving it.

According to an analysis done by a nonpartisan consulting firm retained by the *L.A. Times,* Bush collected "$1.5 million from companies whose aged oil refineries and power plants in Texas have come under pressure to reduce particularly high toxic emissions." That's big money. But the one figure that left us all whomper-jawed is the "$4.5 million from businesses, medical, real estate and other interests that waged a fight, supported by the governor, to make it more difficult to sue Texas firms."

Why does the Republican money trail always lead back to tort reform? In May 1999 R. G. Ratcliffe of the *Houston*

Chronicle teamed up with *Chronicle* political writer and columnist Alan Bernstein to look at the top one hundred donors in Texas politics. Ratcliffe and Bernstein identified all the big funders and came to the following conclusions: "Republicans are mostly business people with known interests in lawsuit reform, reducing taxes and adopting school vouchers. The Democratic donors are dominated by trial lawyers."

No one compares the senior generation of legendary Texas trial lawyers—Warren Burnett, George McAlmon, Malcolm McGregor, Frank Herrera, Pat Maloney, Joe Jamail, et al.—to Mother Teresa. It just so happened that their pecuniary interest—and as hard as it is to imagine in fin de siècle America, their principles—made life more fair for the little people looking to the courts to provide some equity in dealing with the bankers, bullies, and bastards who have always owned and operated the Great State.

Fifteen years ago Republicans recognized that if they could rewrite the rules of civil justice, they could not only buck up the support of the state's big corporate interests, they could cut off the flow of money to Democratic candidates. And by God, they have. But if you think the old civil-justice system in Texas was unfair because it made Joe Jamail a multimillionaire, there's a man in Amarillo who could probably give you a pair of shoes he no longer needs—and tell you which asses need kicking.

Bush never even mentions campaign-finance reform on his own. In April 1999 he announced he favors *raising* the limits on individual contributions. He didn't say by how much, but as John Judis noted in *The New Republic,* Bush had fifty contributors who gave more than $50,000 each to his 1998 gubernatorial campaign. The only consequence of raising individual limits would be to make big money an even bigger player in politics. And when Bush was pressed to say what he'd do about soft money, he said he'd ban contributions from corporations and labor unions but impose no limit on individual soft-money contributions. Again, the result would be to give still more leverage to the very wealthy, like the $100,000 Republican contributors called "Team 100," or the Democrats' similar group, "Team 2000."

The end result of Bush's wretched proposals for "reform" would be to give an almost infinitely larger voice to people like James Leininger, Richard Mellon Scaife, Steve Forbes, and all the rest on the Fortune 500 list. As our economy keeps producing greater and greater distortions in income distribution—every study shows the rich have become vastly more rich while everybody else is stuck in place—Bush's proposal means the end of democracy and a direct leap into oligopoly, rule by the rich. One of the oldest sayings in politics is "You got to dance with them what brung you." The late H. L. Hunt, one of our battier Texas billionaires, once wrote a book in which he proposed that people be allowed to vote according to how much money they have: The more money you had, the more votes you would get. H.L. would have loved the Bush system.

Juntos Podemos: Bush and the Rio Grande Valley

I want prosperity to spread its wings all across America.
I don't want to see anybody left behind.
—Governor George W. Bush

Entre dicho y hecho, hay un gran trecho.
(Between the word and the deed lies a big trench.)
—Mexican proverb

From the front door of Carmen Anaya's tiny grocery store in Las Milpas, Texas, you can see a lot of somebodies being left behind. Six miles to the south is a new bridge across the Rio Grande, built to accommodate the truck traffic that began to swell after the North American Free Trade Agreement was signed. Eight miles to the north is the county seat of one of the poorest places in the United States. East and west, along what Anaya refers to as *las orillas del río,* or the river's banks, are hundreds of *colonias,* "subdivisions" where developers never got around to providing the streets, sewers, and drinkable water they promised when they sold the lots, carried the notes, and then moved on to the next instant slum. Families who buy lots in the *colonias* build their houses of whatever materials they can afford on day-laborer or migrant-farmworker wages. Crop dusters wash the adjacent fields with herbicides and pesticides. School buses stop at the end of the blacktop rather than risk the rutted, muddy roads running with sewage in these rural slums.

Porfirio Díaz, the Mexican dictator, said one hundred years ago that his country was *"tan cerca de los Estados Unidos y tan lejos de Díos."* ("So close to the United States, so far from God.") Flip the adjectives and you have the Rio Grande Valley of Texas. If the forty-two border-region counties along the *orillas del río* were a separate nation, they'd look like a Central American republic. In 1998, comptroller John Sharp issued a two-hundred-page report on the border. He found that if it were the fifty-first state, it would be:

☆ first in poverty (29.5 percent)
☆ first in the rate of unemployment (8 percent)
☆ first in the number of schoolchildren living in poverty (38 percent)
☆ first in the percentage of adults without a high school diploma (37 percent)
☆ forty-fifth in the percentage of adults with a college degree (10.3 percent)
☆ forty-sixth in average annual pay ($22,541)
☆ forty-ninth in percentage of households without a telephone (87 percent)
☆ fifty-first in per capita income ($15,570)
☆ third in female-headed families (14.2 percent)
☆ third in percentage of foreign-born population (14 percent)
☆ first in birth rate (twenty-one births per 1,000).

The people here constitute the largest segment of Texas' working poor. They work, but that doesn't get them out of poverty. Note that 86 percent of them are native-born Americans. Many come from families who were here long before Stephen F. Austin brought in the first party of Anglo settlers. Some of their forebears fought at the Alamo and in the War of Independence; they fought in the Spanish-American War, World War I, World War II, Korea, Vietnam, and the Persian Gulf. They have the highest number of Medal of Honor winners of any ethnic group.

The border region is so desperately in need of public money and infrastructure that one highly regarded Republican state senator called for a "Marshall Plan to save it." But in spite of back-to-back budget surpluses exceeding $10 billion in the 1997 and 1999 legislative sessions, there is no evidence that George W. Bush ever considered a coordinated plan for the Valley or any other stretch of the border. What he wanted was big tax cuts in a state that already ranks fiftieth in per capita state spending.

"He doesn't veto any of our stuff. That's the best we can say about him," said Sister Judy Donovan, who works with Valley Interfaith, a church-based advocacy group that includes forty-nine congregations in the five counties of the lower Rio Grande Valley. She added that over the past four years Bush has provided $1.6 million from his discretionary funds to a regional job-training program Valley Interfaith lobbied to establish. But one job-training program is not a Marshall Plan.

Valley Interfaith was founded by Ernesto Cortés, a Saul Alinsky–trained organizer from the Industrial Areas Foundation. Cortés' work in building a dozen regional advocacy groups in Texas has earned him a MacArthur Foundation "genius grant" and numerous other awards. No one doubts that the group has changed the political landscape of the

Valley. Carmen Anaya, who has watched Texas politics for forty years, says of the days before Valley Interfaith began organizing there, "It was always the same story. They came with promises, left with our votes, and we never saw them again, these officials who were supposed to be working for us." Anaya, an Interfaith leader, says that since the eighties, Valley Interfaith has been working on a Marshall Plan of its own. They have done it the old-fashioned way: by paying attention, organizing, and showing up. Valley Interfaith's citizen lobbyists frequently line up at 4:00 A.M. to pile onto chartered buses for the six-hour trip to Austin to meet with legislators, the governor, the attorney general, the education commissioner, and the state's water-and-sewer bureaucrats. At 5:00 P.M., when government offices close, they board the buses for the trip home. And they have been successful, though there are still many *colonias* that lack water, streets, or sewers. But *colonias* with *no* public services are—to borrow a phrase from former House speaker Gib Lewis— "far and few between."

Not as far and few between as W. Bush's working visits to the area. *"Todos. Todos vinieron,"* said Anaya. "They all came. Mark White came. *La Gobernadora Anna* came and walked in the mud with her fine boots. Henry Cisneros, Bill Hobby, Jim Hightower. They made promises and they fulfilled them," she said of governors and other officials who held office just before Bush. To Anaya it is not a matter of partisan politics. When Senator Kay Bailey Hutchison visited the area in April 1999, Anaya accompanied her. "She walked into a house with rotten plywood floors. She walked through the mud streets while it was raining." (Hutchison also helped secure $3 million in federal funding for the *colonias,* Anaya said.)

The politicians come to tour the *colonias* and attend "accountability sessions" held by Valley Interfaith and its sister organizations around Texas. At these sessions for candidates and elected officials, the group's agenda is stated and politicians are asked for a simple yes or no on their support for each of the issues. W. Bush is an exception; he has never been to an accountability session with Valley Interfaith or its sister organizations in El Paso and San Antonio. Bush did have one preliminary meeting with this, the most important Hispanic organization in Texas, before his first campaign: Cortés and a few Valley Interfaith leaders and organizers met Bush in his executive office at the Ballpark at Arlington.

Bush's point man on border affairs, Secretary of State Elton Bomer, made one highly publicized tour of the border. "He came down here once," said Carmen's son, Eddie Anaya, a lawyer and second-generation Valley Interfaith leader. "Later I saw his assistant when I was in Austin and asked him where he'd been. 'I've been pretty busy,' was his answer. They don't seem to have much interest in the *colonias* issue."

These official visits to the border are more than grip-and-grin photo ops. Providing services for the *colonias* is a protracted process. Before Bush became governor, the Lege—prodded by Valley Interfaith—passed a bill to provide water and sewer facilities for the border *colonias*. Money was approved by voters in bond issues in 1989 and 1991. And "model-subdivision rules" were put in place to stop developers from creating new *colonias* while old ones were being upgraded. But getting the job done requires the collaboration of the attorney general, two state agencies, county authorities, and contractors. The governor is the only one in a position to get all the agencies to work together, and he's been a no-show.

"Everyone thought Bush owed the border something for

the Hispanic turnout in the last election," said a veteran border reporter. "All we got was a few crumbs." Senator David Sibley's Marshall Plan for the Valley passed the Senate but died in the House, in part because Bush was too busy with his presidential campaign to pay much attention to the Lege. "There was a sense that it would have been different if Bush had been there," the reporter said. "But there was nobody to push the border legislation in the House."

What the border got from the Legislature was three "one-stop inspection stations" that will speed up the long lines of NAFTA trucks. Bush is a cheerleader for NAFTA and free trade in general. NAFTA has benefited bankers and dealmakers in Houston and Dallas, but on the border it is a net loss. Lost jobs, traffic jams, and increased costs for highway repairs are the only benefits of NAFTA. In El Paso, the largest city on the border, more than 10,000 "NAFTA casualties" signed up for Transitional Adjustment Assistance, a $7,500 stipend that allows workers to "retool" after they lose their jobs because their factories have shut down and moved to Mexico. Cindy Arnold, who works with displaced garment workers in El Paso, called the program "a fraud" because all it does is take workers who had been making $10 a hour at Levi's plants and prepare them for minimum-wage jobs in the service sector. The needle trades, which provided decent wages by border standards, have disappeared. Less than a month after Bush lauded NAFTA in his State of the State address, Levi's announced its final round of plant closings—13,000 jobs lost over two years.

Many of the jobs are not actually lost; they have just been moved across the border to the *maquiladoras,* the American-owned companies that pay an average of $1.36 an hour in factories located a few miles south of the Rio Grande.

There, workers assemble products for sale in the U.S.—for companies that pay almost no import tax. Manufacturing jobs in the *maquila* zone have increased by 222,000 since 1994. Bill Clinton pushed NAFTA through the Senate, and Ann Richards supported it; it is not Bush's creation. The capital and job flight to Mexico began before he was elected, but the consequences for the border should be his concern.

The "free-trade zone" on the Mexican side has done more than displace American workers. American-owned plants just a few miles beyond the reach of the EPA have produced devastating environmental consequences. Volatile organic compounds, solvents, and heavy metals often end up in the ditches of the huge industrial parks, and the vast dump at Matamoros, just across the river from Brownsville, is an often-smoldering industrial waste site.

In the late 1980s, public-health clinics on the U.S. side began to notice a high incidence of babies born with neural-tube defects—spina bifida or anencephaly—congenital defects that leave parts of the spinal cord or brain exposed or undeveloped. (The tabloid press refers to anencephalic infants as BABIES WITH NO BRAINS!) In 1993 Brownsville attorney Tony Martínez sued General Motors, Zenith, AT&T, and a long list of less well-known corporations on behalf of the parents of the deformed babies, claiming toxins released by *maquiladoras* owned by the American companies caused the birth defects.

Martínez brought General Motors, the last holdout in the case, to settlement by sending the company lawyers a videotape. Not of the permanently disabled children, or the burning piles of waste in the Matamoros dump, or the toxic-smoke plumes from the *maquilas* just upwind of the children's homes. The videotape simply recorded Tejanos going

about their business on the streets and in the town plaza of
Brownsville. Martínez told the corporate lawyers and executives, "Gentlemen, this is your jury pool." No one in the
jury pool looked anything like the Anglo executives. It was
enough. The thirty *maquilas* sued by Martínez settled for
$17 million, although the plant owners maintained that
the birth defects were caused by other factors, and federal
and state agencies have found no direct cause of the birth
defects.

"These kids have a short life," said Martínez. "But at
least they're off Medicaid and the mothers can stay home
and take care of the kids. The whole deal was to take care
of the kids; they have their mothers with them instead of
nurses, and the government isn't paying for it."

The suit also produced some good public policy. "We fa-
cilitated a cleanup of the air in Matamoros," said Martínez.
"And there was no Birth Defect Registry when we sued.
Now there is." The Lege created the registry in 1993 in response to the lawsuit that had brought attention to the clus-
ter of birth defects on the border.

Cyrus Reed of the Texas Center for Policy Studies in
Austin agreed that the suit made a difference in the region:
"You can't prove the suit forced GM to put in wastewater-
treatment plants. But after the lawsuit, they started building
water-treatment plants and cleaning up their plants." GM
had operated *maquiladoras* on the Mexican side of the border for twenty years before building its first plant to treat
hazardous industrial waste water.

But it is unlikely such a lawsuit will ever be filed again.
By pushing "tort reform" through the Lege in 1995, Bush
helped make large, multiple-defendant torts almost impossible to try. According to Martínez, the standards for expert

scientific witnesses have been set so high that it is almost impossible to prove a case against a polluting defendant. "If you can't prove it to an infinite degree of science, it doesn't happen."

Changes in the rules of joint-and-several liability, meaning collective liability, also make it harder to collect damages, and even if the deck were not stacked against plaintiffs, the shift in political power has discouraged lawyers from taking such cases. "Because of the current Republican leadership and the makeup of the Supreme Court [nine Republicans], it is almost impossible for cases like that to move forward," said Martínez. "The bigger picture of tort reform is that industry and corporate America have been emboldened. They know we have to be lucky to get past the trial court." Meanwhile, neural-tube defects along the border decreased in 1995 and 1997, but there has recently been a slight increase, according to Jorge Treviño, regional director of the Neural Tube Defect Project.

Instead of a Marshall Plan of infrastructure, jobs, and investment in education and the environment, the border got a martial plan—soldiers deployed by the feds along the Rio Grande to stop drugs and illegal immigrants. But there was one Hispanic program for which Bush went all out. "Whatever you say we need to spend, I want you to double it," said Bush. "If you say a million, I want you to spend two million. If you say two million, I want you to spend four million. . . . I want to show Latinos there's a lot of opportunity in Texas." Unfortunately, he wasn't talking to the chairman of the House Appropriations Committee; he was giving orders to Lionel Sosa, the San Antonio adman who did the Spanish-language media campaign in the '98 election. Sosa, who is now working on Spanish media for Bush's presidential campaign, spent the money and helped Bush win a record percentage of Hispanic voters in the '98 election. Interesting how you can solve some problems by spending money.

Six years of George W. Bush's public policy has given Texas austerity budgets in order to provide relatively meaningless tax breaks to property owners. Bush criticized his own party in Washington for trying to balance the federal budget "on the backs of the poor." They might well ask him what he thinks he's been doing in Texas. It was the Lege that insisted on increasing the welfare allowance from $188 to $201 a month for a woman with two children—not Bush, who wanted tax breaks. His legacy comes into sharp focus on the border.

"He could have made a huge difference," said Representative Domingo García. "But he gave the surplus away in tax breaks that amount to a super-size meal at McDonald's." Senator Eliot Shapleigh of El Paso told *USA Today*, "I'm flattered Bush is the first Republican to recognize the Hispanic vote. But it might have more to do with political strategy. . . . If Bush is running on a platform of prosperity in the next millennium and in his own state we have such problems, it's fair to ask him what happened."

Bush's campaign slogan in '98 was *"Juntos podemos"*— "Together we can." A famous typo in the *Houston Chronicle* turned that into *"Juntos pedemos,"* or "Together we fart"—quite a collectors' item.

If all of this leaves you with a sense of confusion over Bush's current incarnation as a champion of the downtrodden, it should. Many are the charming pictures showing him cuddling little brown kids and reading to little black kids; many are the speeches in which he urges us not to forget those left behind "in the shadow of affluence." What's a lot harder to find is any evidence that he's done anything at all as governor of Texas that would make any difference in their lives, except to make them harder. The record is so wildly different from the rhetoric in this area, one can only conclude the rhetoric is pure political hooey. We point out again that poor people in Texas are overwhelmingly workers; $201 a month doesn't encourage welfare queens. Their values have not been corrupted by sixties leftists. They just don't make a living wage, and the programs designed to help them are all but hidden by the state.

George W. Bush is promising to do for the rest of the country what he has done for Texas.

There it is.

ABOUT THE AUTHORS

MOLLY IVINS's column is syndicated to more than two hundred newspapers, from Anchorage to Miami, including her home paper, the *Fort Worth Star-Telegram*. A three-time Pulitzer Prize finalist, she is the former coeditor of *The Texas Observer* and former Rocky Mountain bureau chief for *The New York Times*. She has a B.A. from Smith College and a master's in journalism from Columbia University. Her first book, *Molly Ivins Can't Say That, Can She?* spent more than twelve months on *The New York Times* bestseller list.

LOU DUBOSE has been active in Texas journalism for seventeen years, as both a newspaper reporter and a freelancer, and has covered the Texas Legislature for the past thirteen years. He has a master's degree in Latin American studies. Since 1987, he has been the editor of *The Texas Observer*.

ABOUT THE TYPE

This book was set in Sabon, a typeface designed by the well-known German typographer Jan Tschichold (1902–74). Sabon's design is based upon the original letter forms of Claude Garamond and was created specifically to be used for three sources: foundry type for hand composition, Linotype, and Monotype. Tschichold named his typeface for the famous Frankfurt typefounder Jacques Sabon, who died in 1580.